MURDEROUS MINDS UNITED KINGDOM

MURDEROUS MINDS UNITED KINGDOM

International Serial Killers Encyclopedia

Book 4

ALAN R. WARREN

House of Mystery Publishing

Seattle, Washington, USA

Vancouver, British Columbia, Canada

First Edition

ISBN (Paperback): 978-1-989980-87-3
ISBN (eBook): 978-1-989980-86-6

Cover design, formatting, layout, and editing by Evening Sky Publishing Services

Contents

Book Description

The *International Serial Killers Encyclopedia* series sheds light on the murderous minds of many killers, including their motivations, methods, and madness, through detailed research and explicit retelling of events. Some are notorious names that echo through history books, while others are lesser-known killers whose stories are no less harrowing. Each volume reveals a new layer of darkness.

Monstrous Minds United Kingdom delves into the dark histories of the UK's most infamous murderers from the Victorian era to the present day, as well as some of the lesser-known but equally terrifying criminals. With his signature narrative style, Warren brings to life the twisted minds and heinous acts of killers who have left an indelible mark on British criminal history. His gripping accounts not only recount the gruesome details of their crimes but also offer insights into the psychological, social, and cultural factors that shaped these murderers.

Murderous Minds United Kingdom is more than just a collection of crime stories; it is an exploration of the dark corners of human nature and the enduring fascination with the macabre. Perfect for true crime enthusiasts, historians, and anyone captivated by the complexities of the human mind, this volume is a must-have addition to your bookshelf. Join Alan R. Warren as he unravels the mysteries behind these murderous minds, offering a chilling reminder of the evil that can lurk behind ordinary facades.

Introduction

Welcome to the fourth volume of the *Encyclopedia of International Serial Killers* series, *Murderous Minds United Kingdom*. In this latest installment, we journey across the United Kingdom, delving into the darkest recesses of the human psyche to explore the lives and crimes of some of the most notorious serial killers that have haunted this nation.

The United Kingdom, with its storied history and diverse cultural landscape, has also been the backdrop for some of the most chilling and complex criminal cases in history. From the fog-shrouded streets of Victorian London, where Jack the Ripper's gruesome deeds sparked fear and fascination, to more modern cases that continue to baffle and horrify, this book offers a comprehensive examination of those who have committed acts of extreme violence, often with motives that remain incomprehensible to the ordinary mind.

Alan R. Warren, an established authority in the true crime genre, meticulously presents each case with unparalleled attention to detail. As in the previous volumes, Warren combines in-depth research with compelling storytelling, ensuring that readers understand the facts and gain insight into the twisted minds behind these heinous acts.

Murderous Minds United Kingdom is more than just a catalog of crimes; it is a deep exploration into the nature of evil, the societal factors that can contribute to such behavior, and the enduring impact these individuals have had on the communities they terrorized. Through these pages, the psychological and sociological elements that define the phenomenon of serial killing are focused on while also paying respect to the victims whose lives were tragically cut short.

Whether you are a seasoned true crime enthusiast or a newcomer to the field, this volume offers a gripping and sobering look at the darkest aspects of human nature. Prepare to be both intrigued and disturbed as we uncover the stories of the United Kingdom's most infamous serial killers.

ONE

Amelia Sach & Annie Walters

FINCHLEY BABY FARMERS

Annie Walters' early life remains mysterious, with scant information about her birth or family background. In contrast, more is known about Amelia Sach. Documents shedding light on her early years show that she was baptized as Frances Amelia Thorne on May 5, 1867, in Dorset. It is known that she was the fourth eldest of ten siblings. In 1896, Sach married Jeffrey Sach, a construction worker.

Sach devoted herself to midwifery, eventually establishing a lying-in home for pregnant women seeking assistance during and after childbirth. It also included support for mothers suffering from postpartum depression. By 1900, Sach expanded her services to include adoption facilitation, mainly catering to affluent households wishing to handle pregnancies discreetly.

Annie Walters played a sinister role in Sach's operation. Tasked with disposing of newborns through lethal means, typically morphine poisoning, she deceived mothers by claiming adoption arrangements had been made while charging them fees. Suspicion mounted when Sach's landlord, a police officer residing in Greater London, noticed irregularities in the business. Accordingly, surveillance was initiated on Sach and Walters in 1902.

On November 18, 1902, police intercepted Walters at South Kensington Train Station, discovering a deceased infant in her possession. Both Walters and Sach were arrested, with Walters admitting to administering chlorodyne drops to the baby, allegedly to induce sleep.

However, a medical examination revealed signs of physical trauma, contradicting Walters' claims.

Charged with murder, both women stood trial on January 15, 1903. Evidence found during a police search, including a trove of infant clothing, corroborated the prosecution's case. It was supported by testimony from mothers who had entrusted their infants to Sach and Walters. After a brief deliberation, the jury returned a verdict of murder.

After being sentenced to death, both women were executed. Sach's refusal to walk necessitated her being carried to the gallows. Their double execution was carried out on February 3, 1903. They were interred in unmarked graves on the Holloway Prison grounds but later reburied in a common grave alongside other executed female inmates during prison renovations in 1971.

TWO

George Joseph Smith

BRIDES IN THE BATH

G eorge Joseph Smith was born on January 11, 1872, in Bethnal Green, London, England, and his path veered towards trouble almost from the outset. Due to his delinquent behavior, he enrolled in a reform school by the age of nine.

Following school, he drifted through various occupations, frequently entangled in theft and mischief. In 1896, his criminal tendencies led to his arrest after coaxing a female colleague to embezzle from their employer. It resulted in a year-long prison sentence.

Smith assumed the alias George Oliver Love upon his release, and eventually, he married Caroline Beatrice Thornhill in Leicester. The couple resettled in London, where Thornhill worked as a maid in affluent households. At Smith's behest, she stole valuables from her employers. The thefts led to her incarceration for a year following a conviction. Upon her release in January 1901, she implicated Smith, resulting in a two-year imprisonment for him. Thornhill, fearing Smith's retribution, fled to Canada before his release.

In 1908, Smith embarked on a spree of bigamous marriages, entering into unions with seven different women over six years. His modus operandi typically involved marrying women, absconding with their assets, and repeating the cycle with new victims in a new city.

His first victim was the widowed Florence Wilson. He parted with a substantial sum. Subsequent marriages to Edith Peglar and Sarah Freeman followed similar patterns of financial exploitation.

In 1910, under the guise of Henry Williams, Smith wed Bessie Mundy. They resided in a home lacking a bathtub, so he rented one. Rumors of Mundy's health issues surfaced, with Smith attributing her ailments to seizures. A local doctor prescribed medication for her purported headaches, but suspicions surrounding Smith's intentions grew.

On July 12, 1912, Williams/Smith reported to the doctor that his wife had suffered another seizure, prompting the doctor to promise a visit the following day. Upon the doctor's arrival, he made a grim discovery: Bessy had drowned in the rented bathtub. Her body lay submerged, her head underwater and legs extended over the tub, but devoid of any apparent signs of violence. While suspicious, her death was deemed accidental. Five days before her death, Bessy updated her will, leaving her entire estate of twenty-five hundred pounds to her husband.

In 1913, Smith married Alice Burnham, who was later found by her husband lifeless in her bathtub on December 13th. Alice Smith had also recently procured a life insurance policy before her demise.

The following year, in 1914, Smith married two more women: Alice Reid and Margaret Lofty.

He married Alice Reid under the alias Charles Oliver James and Margaret Lofty under the alias John Lloyd. Margaret was discovered deceased in her Highgate home by her husband and their landlady, apparently drowned in her bathtub just days before Christmas.

Joseph Crossley and his wife, proprietors of a Blackpool apartment building near Alice Smith's demise, grew suspicious. Mrs. Crossley, an avid newspaper reader, noted the striking resemblance between Margaret Lofty's and Alice Smith's deaths. After relentless urging from his wife, Crossley composed a letter to the police detailing the suspicious circumstances surrounding both deaths. It included newspaper clippings and was sent on January 3, 1915.

Chief Inspector Arthur Neil of the Metropolitan Police launched an investigation, initially examining Margaret Lofty's residence and questioning the plausibility of her drowning in the small bathtub. He consulted the medical examiner, who found no signs of foul play except for a single bruise on Lofty's elbow.

Further inquiry revealed both victims had hastily altered their wills shortly before their deaths, with significant life insurance policies taken out in their names. When Neil uncovered that Smith's life insurance policy on his deceased wife mirrored the circumstances of the other woman's death, suspicion heightened. Smith's attempt to claim insurance prompted Neil to detain him for questioning on charges of bigamy and suspicion of murder.

Margaret Lofty's exhumation and examination by Dr. Spilsbury from the Home Office provided compelling evidence suggesting foul play. Dr. Spilsbury noted a peculiar aspect of the drownings, as rapid loss of consciousness upon submersion is atypical in most drowning cases. To explore potential causes, Spilsbury ordered blood tests to detect any signs of poisoning and examined them for indications of heart disease. But no evidence surfaced.

Chief Inspector Neil orchestrated an untried approach to the investigation. He relocated the bathtub to the police station for repeated reenactments of the drownings. The ensuing tests captured widespread attention, becoming headline news across the nation.

On February 8th, the police chief of Herne Bay, spurred by the sensational reports, initiated an inquiry into a similar bathtub-related death in his jurisdiction. The victim, Bessie Mundy, had been married to George Joseph Smith in 1910 and was found drowned in her bathtub. A death that always seemed suspicious to him.

To ascertain if the George Joseph Smith in custody was the same individual married to Bessie Mundy, Neil dispatched photographs of Smith to the Herne police chief. Confirmation swiftly arrived, affirming their identity match.

Dr. Spilsbury concluded his examination, resolving that all three women had been drowned through a method involving forceful submersion, causing rapid loss of consciousness. Consequently, on March 23, 1915, George Joseph Smith faced formal charges for the murders of Alice Smith, Margaret Lofty, and Bessie Mundy.

Smith's trial commenced on June 22, 1915, at the Old Bailey Court, spanning approximately three weeks. He was ultimately convicted and sentenced to death.

Despite a subsequent appeal filed by his defense counsel, the verdict stood. On August 13, 1915, George Joseph Smith met his fate at Maidstone Prison, where he was executed by hanging.

THREE

Gordon Cummins

THE BLACKOUT KILLER

Gordon Frederick Cummins was the eldest of four siblings born on February 18, 1914, in New Earswick, North Yorkshire, England. His father, John Cummins, managed a school that catered to troubled youth entangled with the law. Gordon and his siblings received their education at a private school in South Wales.

Cummins earned his chemistry diploma at the age of sixteen in 1930. He enrolled at Northampton College of Technology in the Autumn of that year but abandoned his studies by November 1932. After that, he relocated to Newcastle and secured employment as an industrial chemist. However, his tenure only lasted five months due to concerns over his socialization during work hours and failure to complete assigned tasks.

In August 1933, Cummins transitioned to a job in Northampton involving tanning animal hides and skins. This employment ceased after a year, as Cummins frequently skipped work without reason. Subsequently, he was employed in short-term positions on various small-scale projects.

In October 1934, Cummins settled in London as a leather worker in a clothing factory, earning a weekly salary of three pounds. He eventually climbed to a supervisory role, demonstrating more excellent proficiency.

While in London, Cummins immersed himself in the city's upscale hotels and clubs, which were predominantly frequented by the affluent. Adopting an aristocratic façade, he often masqueraded as the illegitimate child of nobility or royalty, regaling others with tales of his Oxford education. However, his modest income failed to sustain his lavish lifestyle, prompting Cummins to commit theft and embezzlement.

Struggling to maintain his deceptive lifestyle, Cummins' poor performance at work led to his dismissal in 1935. His downward spiral became apparent when he was forced to seek refuge in his brother's apartment in Queen's Mews, Bayswater.

Cummins next enlisted in the Royal Air Force stationed in Regent's Park, London. Following his assessment, he was directed to training as an aircraft rigger. He earned praise from officers for his ambition and diligent work ethic, although his fellow soldiers were put off by his constant boasting of noble lineage, and they mockingly dubbed him "The Duke."

Sometime during his service, Cummins crossed paths with Marjorie Stevens, a secretary to a theater producer in the West End, and they embarked on a romantic relationship. Despite a quick seven-month courtship, the couple were married on December 28, 1936. Cummins was reassigned to Scotland to contribute to a military research team.

With the onset of World War II in 1939,

Cummins was deployed to the base at Helensburgh, Dunbartonshire, where he remained until April 1941. He was then transferred to Colerne, Wiltshire, where he attained the rank of leading aircraftsman.

Cummins was later stationed in Cornwall on November 10, 1941, where his penchant for regaling fellow soldiers with tales of his purported noble lineage earned him the nickname "The Count." Undeterred, he pursued becoming a Spitfire pilot, eventually amassing the requisite one thousand hours of flying to qualify for the aviation test. Cummins was passing with flying colors and found himself stationed alongside three hundred other airmen at the Air Crew Receiving Center in Regent's Park by February 1942. Meanwhile, Cummins and his wife had secured an apartment in Southwark, enabling his visits during leaves from duty.

On February 8, 1942, Cummins borrowed a pound from his wife and ventured out with fellow airmen for a drink in the West End. The following day, an electrician named Harold Batchelor stumbled upon the lifeless body of Evelyn Hamilton, a forty-year-old pharmacist, in a street-level air raid shelter in Montagu Place. The scene bore signs of a violent struggle, with Hamilton's clothing torn and broken pieces of mortar scattered around her. Her handbag, emptied and strewn across the area, offered no clues, as police could not recover any fingerprints from the scene or her possessions.

Police learned that Hamilton had worked managing a drug store in Hornchurch. But since the war started, they had hit hard times, and she had resigned the day before. She was moving to Lincolnshire for a new job at a different drugstore doing the same thing. A waitress last saw her around midnight near to where she was found. The medical examiner determined that she had died due to strangulation, probably carried out by a lefthanded person. Hamilton had not been sexually assaulted in any way.

Two days later, around eight-thirty in the morning, two meter readers entered the apartment of thirty-four-year-old Evelyn Oatley in Soho. They found her dead, lying naked on her bed with her head hanging over the edge. Police arrived shortly after and began their investigation. The medical examiner determined that Oatley's throat had been cut so deeply that it severed her carotid artery. His stomach, genitals, and legs had been mutilated after she was dead. They also figured that because of the way the wounds had been inflicted, it was probably done with a can opener. She had also been sexually assaulted with an electric torch that had been left in her vagina. Several razor blades were next to her head, and a bloody curling iron was found nearby.

The door to her apartment was closed but not locked when she was found. The killer had gone through her purse, and most of her possessions had been thrown around the apartment. Oatley had no defensive wounds or marks on her hands or arms, and there was nothing found under her nails.

Detectives found some fingerprints among some of the bloodstains and a broken mirror in her apartment. It was determined that the murderer was also left-handed. After a search of police files, they could not find a match to the prints they had seen in their database.

Oatley was married at the time of the murder, but her husband was away fighting in the war, leaving her alone. Detectives learned that she ended up prostituting herself to make enough money to survive. She was last seen at a club the night before she was found dead and was with an airman with chestnut brown hair. At about eleven that night, her neighbor had also seen Oatley returning home with a man with a similar description.

On February 13th, fifteen-year-old Barbara Lowe came from a boarding school in London to visit her mother, Margaret Florence Lowe, who was a forty-three-year-old prostitute. Barbara could not get an answer at her mother's apartment. A neighbor came out into the hallway when she heard the girl knocking on the door and told her that her mother hadn't been home for two days. Upset by this, Barbara went to see the landlady to find out if she knew where her mother might have gone.

The landlady said she didn't know where Barbara's mother was and that a package had been left outside her door for a couple of days. The two of them decided to go into the apartment and see if they could find anything showing where she went.

Lowe's body was discovered, wrapped in several blankets, and placed under her bed. She was lying on her back with her legs apart, and knees bent upwards toward the bottom of the bed. Nylons had been tied tightly around her neck, and fluid could be seen coming from her nose and mouth.

Police learned that Lowe was last seen walking

into her apartment in the morning on February 11th with a man thought to have been a customer by one of her other neighbors, Florence Bartolini. She also heard the client leave because he loudly whistled as he walked out of Lowe's apartment and down the hallway.

The medical examiner determined that Lowe had been beaten badly and, like the two previous victims, had also been mutilated. In Lowe's case, her mutilation was much more aggressive, and most of it was done while she was still alive. The killer had used many more items during his attack on Lowe, including a kitchen knife, razor blades, a table knife, and even a fire poker, which was left stabbed into her body. A six-inch candle was placed into her vagina and left there as well.

Several fingerprints were found at the crime scene, and again, the attacker was thought to be lefthanded. However, like the other fingerprints found at the different crime scenes, no records matched them.

On February 12th, Catherine Mulcahy, a twenty-five-year-old prostitute, was approached by Cummins, who offered her two pounds to have sex with her. After she agreed and received the money, the pair took a taxi to her apartment. After they entered her place, she lit the gas fire, removed her clothing except for her boots, got onto the bed, and told him to come over. She decided not to remove her boots as she didn't like the expression and smile that Cummins had on his face when she was getting naked.

Cummins approached the bed and removed his clothing, then lay on top of her. Suddenly, he kicked her stomach with his knee and began to strangle her with his hands. Mulcahy was able to kick him in his crotch with her boot, which hurt him enough that he let go of her throat, and she fell onto the floor beside the bed. She got up, ran, screamed at the top of her lungs, and reached her neighbor's house. Cummins quickly got half-dressed and followed her to the neighbor's house. He threw some money at her and said that he was sorry, claiming that he had too much to drink. But she continued to scream, so he fled the house.

Instead of Cummins going home after his attack on Mulcahy, he returned downtown to look for another victim. He found Doris Jouannet, a thirty-two-year-old prostitute. She was drinking with her friend, Beatrice Lang, at a local tearoom before meeting her customer, whom she called "The Captain." She met Cummins and took him to her apartment in Bayswater, where she lived with her husband.

The next day, Jouannet's husband returned home to find the bedroom door locked. He was unable to open the door, so he called the police. When the officer arrived, he told the husband to wait in the hallway. When he broke into the bedroom, he found Jounnet dead. She was lying on the bed with a silk stocking wrapped tightly around her neck and her hand between her legs.

Like the previous victims, Jouannet's body had been badly mutilated in several places. Her stomach, genitals, legs, and left breast all had been cut with a razor blade or knife. The flesh beneath her left breast had been cut away and removed from her body. Two used condoms were left on the floor in the bedroom. One thing different in this case was the victim's jaw had been broken. Spilsbury was the medical examiner on Jouannet's case, and he determined that her breast injury was done before she died, while all the other injuries were committed after she died.

During the war, the amount of press on local events, including murders, was limited. But with so many murders happening within a short period within the West End of London, it wasn't long before everyone was talking about them. Soon, the murders were dubbed "The Blackout Murders," and prostitutes began seeing only their regular customers and no longer taking new ones.

Even with all the attention focused on the "Blackout Killer," Cummins continued his attacks. On February 13, 1942, he met Margaret Heywood in London, and the two had a sandwich and drink. The couple then walked towards the Haymarket when suddenly Cummins pushed Heywood into a doorway of a business and started to grope and fondle her. Cummins tried to get Heywood to accompany him to a nearby air raid shelter. She told him that if he stopped, she would let him kiss her. After they kissed, she told him that she didn't think there was an air raid shelter anywhere here, and even if there were one, she wouldn't go with him there anyway.

Cummins got angry and grabbed her again and started touching her again. She began to fight back and tried to leave, but he grabbed her by the throat and choked her until she passed out. As she was losing consciousness, she remembered him saying, "You won't?"

As Cummins rummaged through Heywood's purse, John Shine and an eighteen-year-old delivery boy stumbled upon them at the doorway. Upon being discovered, Cummins hastily fled the scene.

Shine attended to Heywood, and she gradually regained consciousness. He escorted her toward the nearby hospital. En route, they encountered a policeman to whom they recounted the incident before being accompanied to the police station to give a formal statement.

Cummins recollected leaving behind his gas mask and haversack during the assault on Heywood. Realizing they bore his military identification, he was determined to retrieve them. He decided to steal another serviceman's gear from a nearby bar before returning to the base.

But Shine had already retrieved the abandoned gas mask and haversack and handed them over to the police officer upon arrival at the station. The detective promptly contacted the Air Force, disclosing the identity number on the haversack. It confirmed the owner was Cummins.

On February 14th, authorities detained Cummins for interrogation. He vehemently denied any wrongdoing, claiming he had spent every evening socializing with fellow airmen, frequently indulging in alcohol. He vaguely recalled conversing with a woman at a bar on Baker Street after a few rounds of whiskey, admitting his memory faltered. Cummins insisted he returned promptly to the base upon realizing he had exceeded curfew, expressing remorse for any potential harm caused and offering compensation.

Detectives observed a cut on Cummins's left knuckles, which he attributed to an engine repair mishap. He was compelled to provide a written statement, which he signed, before being apprehended on charges of inflicting bodily harm and confined to jail.

Police scrutinized the Air Force base's attendance records, noting several instances coinciding with the times of the attacks and murders where Cummins was logged in. Suspicions were raised by the discovery that Cummins' entries were frequently in pencil, unlike his peers who predominantly used ink. It suggested a possibility for alterations.

Upon questioning other airmen, signing in or out for others to avoid repercussions seemed a common practice. Testimonies indicated that Cummins had prolonged absences from the base during the week of the murders. Additional evidence surfaced when fellow airman Felix Sampson declared they had left by climbing down the fire escape around midnight on the dates of the murders.

A thorough search of Cummins' belongings

on the base uncovered several items belonging to the victims, notably a cigarette lighter engraved with the initials LW, attributed to Evelyn Oatley. Investigators also matched Cummins' fingerprints to those recovered from three crime scenes. Moreover, two surviving victims, Heywood and Mulcahy, positively identified Cummins from a police lineup, further solidifying the case against him.

On February 17th, Cummins faced charges for the murders of Oatley, Lowe, and Jouannet. A week later, he was additionally charged with the murder of Evelyn Hamilton. He was held in custody at HM Prison Brixton until his trial.

The trial for Cummins' first murder charge, that of Evelyn Oatley, commenced on April 24, 1942. Pleading not guilty, Cummins opted to testify in his defense, taking the stand on April 27th. He claimed that he had been with a different woman on the night of Oatley's murder.

The trial concluded on April 28th, with the jury retiring to deliberate at four o'clock. Within thirty minutes, they returned with a guilty verdict.

After being sentenced to death by hanging, Cummins appealed against the verdict. The appeal was dismissed in early June 1942.

On June 25th, Cummins was executed at

Wandsworth Prison. Remarkably, during Cummins' execution, London was subjected to a German air raid, making him the sole prisoner in British history to be executed during such an event.

The other murders attributed to the Blackout Killer were formally linked to Cummins. Scotland Yard also suspected his involvement in two additional murders in Cornwall in 1941.

FOUR

Graham Young

THE TEACUP POISONER

G raham Frederick Young was born on September 7, 1947, in Neasden, Middlesex, England. He had an elder sister named Winifred, and together, they lived with their parents, Frederick and Bessie. When Graham was only fourteen weeks old, tragedy struck, and his mother succumbed to tuberculosis. Following her death, Graham was sent to live with his uncle and aunt, while Winifred went to stay with their grandparents. After his father remarried a few years later, both siblings returned home to live with their father and new stepmother.

From a young age, Graham harbored a fascination with magic and poisons. Over time, his curiosity extended to Adolf Hitler's interest in the occult and the Nazi Party. In 1959, by age twelve, Graham delved into the advanced study of toxicology and poisoning with fervor.

Two years later, a local chemist discovered Graham's interest in toxicology and decided to provide him with antimony, a formerly medicinal substance that was now classified as a registered poison. In 1961, Graham signed the registry to obtain the antimony using the pseudonym M.E. Evans.

Within a month, Graham commenced experiments by administering small doses of poison to various family members. In February of that year, he dosed his stepmother Molly's coffee, causing her severe stomach pain and vomiting, which she attributed to a gallbladder issue.

Graham also administered the poison to his father, who experienced milder symptoms, necessitating a brief period of bed rest.

During the summer, Graham escalated his experiments on his sister, inducing sickness on multiple occasions. To deflect suspicion, he also poisoned himself, feigning illness. Graham went so far as to distribute the poison to some of his schoolmates, causing them to fall ill and thereby creating the illusion of a viral outbreak in the town.

In November 1961, Graham prepared tea for his sister, Winifred, before she left for work. Upon tasting the tea, Winifred found it excessively bitter and discarded it. However, during her train journey to work, she experienced hallucinations and became unable to disembark until railway workers intervened and brought her to the hospital. Medical examination revealed she had been exposed to Belladonna, a highly toxic substance. When Graham's father learned of Winifred's poisoning, he confronted Graham, who vehemently denied any involvement. Despite his denial, suspicion lingered, prompting a search of his room but yielding no evidence that he was involved.

The Christmas holidays passed without any

further incidents until Easter weekend in April 1962, when Graham's stepmother died at home. Her death followed a car accident a week prior, which was believed to have exacerbated a preexisting disc prolapse condition, ultimately leading to her death.

During the funeral, Graham spiked a jar of mustard pickles with antimony poison, causing several guests, including his father, to fall ill. Concerned by his deteriorating condition, Graham's aunt rushed her brother to the hospital, where doctors confirmed a nearly fatal antimony poisoning. The incident raised suspicions about Graham and prompted his aunt to inform his science teacher, and vials of various poisons were then found in his possession. Subsequently, Graham underwent psychiatric evaluation, leading to his arrest on May 23, 1962.

During interrogation, Graham confessed to poisoning his father, stepmother, sister, and schoolmate. Diagnosed with a psychopathic disorder, he was recommended for admission to Broadmoor Hospital. At his trial, Graham pleaded guilty to the poisonings and received a sentence of fifteen years minimum to be served at Broadmoor.

At only 14 years of age, Grahman Young was the youngest inmate at Broadmoor. While there, he managed to continue his toxicology studies by reading books obtained from Broadmoor's library. He even managed to continue his experiments. But he eventually drew suspicion after a fellow prisoner died from cyanide poisoning. The poisoning raised concerns since cyanide could be extracted from laurel leaves, which were abundant on the hospital grounds. As well, Young's fascination with Naziism and Hitler persisted at Broadmoor, evident in his adoption of Hitler's appearance and mannerisms. It underscored his deeply troubled psyche.

After eight years in Broadmoor, Young was released. It was believed he was no longer obsessed with poisons. A couple of weeks later, he visited a pharmacy in an attempt to purchase poison but was refused due to lack of authorization. Undeterred, he returned a few days later armed with a note with the Bedford College letterhead on it permitting him to procure toxic substances. With this endorsement, he acquired twenty-five grams of antimony potassium tartrate, followed by another purchase of twenty-five grams of thallium.

Moving to a hostel in Slough for a retail management course, Young befriended fellow tenant Trevor Sparkes. Their frequent outings to a local pub abruptly ended when Sparkes fell ill during one of their drinking sessions. Though he eventually recovered, Sparkes experienced recurring bouts of sickness over the next two months. His sickness prompted his return home, where he regained his health over time.

Young managed to secure a position as assistant manager at John Hadland Laboratories in Bovingdon, Hertfordshire, close to his sister's house. The lab specialized in producing military-grade equipment like infrared lenses, necessitating the occasional procurement of thallium bromide-iodide from a chemist in London. To gain access to toxic materials, Young submitted an application concealing his past association with poisons and incarceration at Broadmoor. Instead, he disclosed a fabricated history of personal tragedy. He claimed his lack of employment history was because he suffered a nervous breakdown after the death of his mother. He even had references from Broadmoor that backed up his recovery and rehabilitation and made no mention of his being incarcerated there or his penchant for poisons.

Assigned to serve beverages during work

hours, Young used labeled mugs to ensure correct distribution. Shortly after his employment commenced, a mysterious illness swept through the laboratory, sparking rumors of water contamination from a nearby Air Force base. In June 1971, Young's supervisor, Bob Egle, fell ill with symptoms mirroring those afflicting his coworkers. Despite initially recovering, Egle's condition deteriorated rapidly, leading to his hospitalization and subsequent death from Guillain-Barre syndrome. Young, attending Egle's funeral, grieved his death from what he described as a rare viral infection.

Another worker at the laboratory, Ron Hewitt, who had secured employment elsewhere, also fell ill, albeit less severely than Egle. Fortunately, he recuperated after leaving his position with the lab. Following Egle's funeral, Young was promoted to fill his shoes as supervisor. Given his contentious relationship with colleague Diana Smart, it was a role he reluctantly assumed. To alleviate the tension between them, Young resorted to administering small doses of poison to Smart, inducing mild symptoms to keep her at bay without drawing undue attention following Egle's demise.

By October 1971, Young escalated his

poisoning efforts, targeting coworkers David Tilson and Jethro Batt. Despite his close friendship with Batt, Young spiked his tea with excessive amounts of thallium acetate, rendering the concoction unbearably sweet. Both Tilson and Batt consumed enough to warrant hospitalization due to chest pains, breathing difficulties, numbness in their limbs, and more. They both eventually recovered, but the poisoning left them permanently impotent.

A third poisoning incident at the laboratory, for which Young was culpable, involved fifty-six-year-old part-time employee Fred Biggs. After consuming his afternoon tea on October 30th, he began experiencing dizziness and nausea, making it difficult for him to walk. When his symptoms persisted the following day, he sought medical attention. Even with treatment, his condition rapidly deteriorated. Within a week, Biggs lost the ability to speak, and his skin began to peel off his body. Tragically, Biggs succumbed to his sickness on November 19, 1991.

Following Biggs' death, management at Hadland Lab initiated a formal inquiry into the string of illnesses and deaths among employees. During the investigation, it emerged that Young was the only one to have never fallen ill. It led to speculation that he might have been a carrier of the virus plaguing the lab. Also, some employees divulged Young's fixation on poisons and toxicology, mentioning his habit of reading that kind of literature during lunch breaks.

Lab management alerted the authorities to their findings, prompting a police investigation into the series of incidents at the lab. Detectives realized that all the illnesses and deaths had occurred since Young's employment began, prompting a background check of Young. A more detailed look uncovered his prior history of poisonings and confinement at Broadmoor.

On November 20, 1971, Young was arrested, and a search of his room yielded several bottles of poison, including thallium, antimony, atropine, aconitine, and digitalis. Additionally, police found Nazi symbols and the party leaders' posters adorning his walls. Most damningly, Young's diary contained an admission of his guilt. It detailed each victim and the amount of poison administered.

When confronted, Young confessed to poisoning five employees with thallium. He also boasted about murdering his stepmother, Molly Young. During interrogation, he told investigators that he viewed his victims as mere subjects for experimentation. He was devoid of any empathy for poisoning people.

Graham Young's trial started on June 19, 1972, at the St. Albans Crown Court, where he faced charges of murder, attempted murder, and administering poison with intent to harm. Young pleaded not guilty, but his defense crumbled under the weight of seventy-five witnesses for the prosecution and concrete medical evidence linking thallium to the victims' remains.

The trial lasted ten days, and the jury deliberated for less than two hours before returning a verdict of guilty on two counts of murder (Biggs and Egle), two counts of attempted murder (Batt and Tilson), and two counts of attempted murder with intent to injure (Smart and Hewitt.) However, he was acquitted of poisoning Sparkes and Buck, and the charges related to administering poison with intent to cause grievous bodily harm.

Young, averse to returning to Broadmoor Hospital, received court approval to serve out his life sentence at Park Lane Hospital in Maghull. Coincidentally, convicted child serial murderer and rapist Ian Brady was also housed there, and the two formed a friendship based on their shared fascination with Hitler and the Nazis.

At the age of forty-two, Young died in his cell from a heart attack despite having no history of heart disease. Speculation surrounding his death abounded. It was rumored that he died by suicide or at the hands of other prisoners or staff, though no evidence has ever substantiated claims.

FIVE

John Christie

MONSTER OF RILLINGTON PLACE

B orn on April 8, 1899, in Northowram, Yorkshire, England, John Reginald Halliday Christie entered a family dynamic marked by indifference from his father,

Ernest John Christie, a carpenter, and the oppressive influence of his mother and older sisters. With his grandfather, David Halliday, a looming presence until his passing at seventy-five, Christie experienced a shift in perception from fear of the imposing figure to a sense of empowerment upon his departure.

With an IQ of 128, Christie excelled academically, particularly in mathematics and history, while woodworking and participating in the church choir. Upon completing his schooling in 1913, he commenced work as an assistant film projectionist at the local cinema.

Despite his achievements, Christie remained introverted and lacked popularity among his peers. His struggles with impotence when attempting romantic relationships compounded this, earning him mocking nicknames like "Can't do it, Christie."

With the outbreak of World War I in September 1916, Christie enlisted in the British Army. He underwent training with the Derbyshire Regiment in April 1917, serving as an infantryman before being deployed to France a year later as a radioman.

In June 1918, during a hostile assault, Christie sustained injuries from mustard gas exposure and was hospitalized for a month. He alleged prolonged blindness and speechlessness for over three years due to the exposure to the gas. But Christie's claims were refuted by military authorities, who deemed him fit for duty after a month of treatment. It was believed that his ailments were attributed to a personality disorder characterized by exaggerating illnesses or injuries for sympathy.

Christie's military unit was disbanded in October 1919, prompting his return to Halifax, where he married Ethel Simpson on May 10, 1920. He continued to grapple with impotence, however, and resorted to soliciting prostitutes for intimacy. Ethel did become pregnant nonetheless but sadly suffered a miscarriage.

In 1921, Christie secured employment as a postal worker in Halifax. He soon found himself in legal trouble for stealing parcels for financial gain, leading to a three-month jail term beginning April 12, 1921. After his release, he faced fraud and theft charges in January 1923, resulting in a one-year probationary sentence. His penchant for petty crimes continued, and he spent the next few years of his life in and out of prison.

By December 1923, marital strains culminated in Christie and Ethel's separation. Ethel relocated to Sheffield and secured employment at the English Electric Company. Meanwhile, Christie relocated to London, enlisting in the Royal Air Force. However, his military stint was short-lived. He was terminated the following summer due to his involvement in two robbery incidents, earning him another three-month prison sentence.

Upon release, Christie found employment as a truck driver, maintaining it for two years until an altercation with his roommate, Maud Cole, led to a six-month imprisonment in the harsh confines of HM Prison Wandsworth. Christie violently assaulted Cole with a cricket bat. After that, Christie was convicted of auto theft and imprisoned again in November 1933.

While incarcerated for car theft, Christie reconnected with Ethel. Upon his release in January 1934, they reconciled. The couple settled in 10 Rillington Place, initially occupying the smaller, rundown, noisy top-floor apartment before relocating to the ground floor in 1938. Their residence, constructed in 1870, lacked modern amenities, with all apartments sharing an external toilet.

Christie maintained employment as a theater supervisor until the outbreak of World War II in 1939, prompting his enlistment in the War

Reserve Police. Assigned to the Harrow Road Police detachment, Christie became acquainted with Gladys Jones, a colleague with whom he embarked on an affair lasting four years. However, their liaison met a violent end when Jones' husband discovered them in a compromising position upon his return from military service and assaulted Christie.

In August 1943, while Christie's wife was away visiting his family, he went to a bar and met a prostitute, twenty-one-year-old Ruth Fuerst. Christie offered her some money to go back to his apartment to have sex with him. After they were finished, he strangled her to death with a rope that he had hidden under the bed. At first, he put her body under a loose floorboard in his living room. Two nights later, when the other tenants were out for the evening, he buried her in the backyard of the garden.

In 1944, he quit the police reserves and got a job as a factory clerk. His coworker, Muriel Amelia Eady, had chronic bronchitis, and one day in October, Christie told her that he had a cure for bronchitis that he had learned from his mother. He told her that she was welcome to come over and try it out anytime.

On October 7th, she took him up on his offer.

She went to Chrstie's apartment, where he had a sealed jar with a tube coming from the top. He sat her down and told her to breathe in the mixture through the tube. While seated and breathing in the mix, from behind her, Christie inserted another tube from a gas line into the jar. Eady kept on breathing it in and soon passed out. Christie then raped her. After he was finished, he strangled her to death. He buried Eady's body in the garden, right behind the remains of Fuerst, his first murder victim.

Over the Easter long weekend, a married couple, Timothy and Beryl Evans, moved into a top-floor apartment in the same building that Christie lived in. About six months later, in October 1948, they gave birth to their first child, Geraldine. Just over a year later, Timothy told the police that his wife was dead. Police went to their apartment building but were unable to find the body.

After the media heard the story, police felt enough pressure to search not just Evan's apartment but the whole building, including their neighbors, the Christies. In the outside washroom, they discovered Beryl's body, which had been wrapped up in blankets and a tablecloth. Also, within the blankets, they discovered a sixteen-week-old fetus of a male. Upon searching further, police also found Evan's baby daughter. It was apparent that both the mother and daughter had been strangled to death.

Timothy told detectives that Christie had killed his wife after he tried to give her an abortion, but the police didn't believe what he was telling them. They pressured him just to confess that he was the one who committed the murders. Eventually, Timothy confessed and was charged with murder.

The trial of Timothy Evans, solely for the murder of his daughter, commenced on January 11, 1950. By this point, Evans had recanted his earlier confessions, alleging coercion by the police. Christie appeared as the primary witness for the prosecution, alleging frequent and violent conflicts between Evans and his wife. Despite the defense's disclosure of Christie's criminal history to the jury, Evans was convicted of the murder. However, amidst extensive media coverage of the trial, Christie lost his job at the post office following the revelation of his criminal past in newspapers.

In January, Evans lodged an appeal, which was denied. He was executed by hanging on March 9, 1950.

In December 1952, Ethel Christie vanished

without a trace. Christie informed their neighbors that she had gone to visit her family. To maintain the facade with her family, Christie corresponded with Ethel's relatives on her behalf, citing her rheumatism as the reason for her inability to write.

After losing his job, Christie resorted to selling possessions to cover expenses. Initially, he pawned his wife's wedding ring, watch, and jewelry, then sold most of their furniture, retaining only essential items like his mattress, dishes, kitchen table, and chairs. Forging his wife's signature, he drained his wife's bank account and sold her clothing to a thrift store. It later emerged that Christie had strangled his wife while she slept.

In the early months of 1953, Christie committed further atrocities, murdering three more women: Kathleen Maloney, Rita Nelson, and Hectorina MacLennan. Employing his lethal method, he enticed them to inhale a toxic concoction from a jar and tube, rendering them unconscious before strangling them. Maloney was a prostitute he lured to his apartment. After first meeting MacLennan and her boyfriend in a coffee shop, Christie offered them lodging when they expressed financial struggles. As soon as she was alone, he lured her to his apartment. Rita Nelson, a pregnant prostitute, met Christie at the same coffee shop, where he offered her an abortion. He lured her to his apartment and murdered her after intercourse. After the murders, he stowed their bodies in a small alcove behind the back kitchen wall and covered the entrance to the alcove with wallpaper.

Facing eviction for fraudulent room rentals, Christie relocated to a hostel in King's Cross. After he was gone, the landlord made a grim discovery after peeling off the kitchen wallpaper: the bodies of Maloney, MacLennan, and Nelson. Alerting the authorities, they issued a warrant for Christie's arrest.

After the newspapers broke the news about the discovered bodies and the search for Christie began, he promptly vacated the hostel. Evading capture, the days turned into a blur of theater matinees and coffee shops for Christie as he aimlessly wandered through the streets by night, finding sleep wherever he could. On the morning of March 31st, while heading to a coffee shop, Christie attracted the attention of a vigilant police officer who requested his identification, leading to his swift arrest.

During interrogation, Christie acknowledged the gruesome murders of the three women whose bodies were concealed behind the wallpaper in his kitchen. Additionally, he confessed to the strangulation of his wife. As authorities conducted a thorough search of Christie's residence and surrounding property, further human remains were unearthed in his garden. Compelled by these discoveries, Christie was obliged to admit to the additional murders he had committed.

On June 5, 1953, Christie provided a detailed account of how he ended the lives of both Muriel Eady and Ruth Fuerst. He admitted to murdering Beryl Evans as well, a crime for which her husband had been wrongfully convicted and executed. However, he steadfastly denied any involvement in the death of their daughter, Geraldine. This reluctance likely stemmed from his strategic avoidance of alienating the jury by admitting to the killing of a child, as well as safeguarding himself from potential retaliation from fellow inmates.

On June 22, 1953, the trial concerning the demise of Christie's wife, Ethel, began. He entered a plea of insanity, asserting that he bore no responsibility for her death. Following this plea, the court ordered an evaluation of Christie conducted by Dr. Matheson, the psychiatrist at HM Prison Brixton. Dr. Matheson diagnosed

Christie with a hysterical personality but affirmed his sanity and capacity to stand trial.

The trial spanned approximately one week, culminating in a swift conviction for murder after the jury deliberated for less than an hour. The judge delivered a death sentence. Christie chose not to appeal his conviction, and upon review by the Home Secretary, no grounds for reprieve were found.

On July 15, 1953, Christie met his fate with the gallows at HM Prison Pentonville, the execution scheduled for nine in the morning. Following the custom of the era in England, his remains found their rest in an unmarked grave within the prison grounds.

Following Christie's execution, questions arose regarding the conviction of Timothy Evans for the murders of his wife and daughter. The Home Secretary at the time, who had conversed with Christie before his demise, interviewed twenty-five additional witnesses from Evans' original trial. After careful consideration, it was determined that Evans was likely responsible for the deaths.

Despite this conclusion, doubt lingered among

the populace, prompting ongoing nationwide discussions. In the Winter of 1965, the British High Court intervened, undertaking a thorough review of the case evidence. After this examination, the Home Secretary decreed that Timothy Evans deserved a posthumous pardon. Evans' remains were disinterred and returned to his family, who laid him to rest in a private grave.

SIX

John Haigh

ACID BATH MURDERER

On July 24, 1909, John Geoge Haigh was born an only child in Stamford, Lincolnshire, England. His family belonged to the Plymouth Brethren, a conservative protestant church. His father, John

Robert Haigh, worked as an engineer, while his mother, Emily, was a homemaker.

In school, John did well and won a scholarship to attend the Queen Elizabeth Grammar School in Wakefield. He also loved classical music, went to several concerts, learned to play the piano, and became a choir singer for the church.

After completing school, Haigh got a job as an engineer at an automotive company. After working there for about a year, he took a different job in 1930, advertising for an insurance agency. He was fired from that job after money went missing from the change drawer, and the manager believed Haigh likely took it.

In the Summer of 1934, Haigh married Beatrice Hamer, twenty-three. He was now working in the car business. Beatrice became pregnant, but before she gave birth to their baby girl, Haigh was arrested for forging car ownership papers and put in jail. After having the child, Beatrice decided she was going to divorce Haigh and put their baby up for adoption.

Haigh was released from prison in 1936 and moved to London, where he got a job as a driver for William McSwan, owner of several amusement parks. Using the high-end vehicles that belonged to McSwan, Haigh would pretend to be a lawyer, using the fake name of William Cato Adamson. He would sell fake stock shares that were supposed to be from his clients who had recently died. Within a year, he was caught, convicted of fraud, and sentenced to serve four years in prison.

While he was in jail, he read about a French killer who disposed of his victims using sulphuric acid. He hated the people who testified against him and started to have fantasies about murder and dissolving bodies in acid. He experimented on mice he caught in prison.

In early 1943, Haigh was released from prison, and after returning to London, he got a job as an accountant for an engineering firm. After work one night, he went to a pub for a beer and ran into McSwan, the man he used to drive for. McSwan was out drinking with his parents, Donald and Amy McSwan, who he also worked for by collecting rent from their London properties.

Haigh didn't like McSwan and was jealous of his lifestyle. So, on September 6, 1944, he invited McSwan to his place for a drink, intent on killing him. As soon as McSwan entered, Haigh hit him over the head with a lead pipe. He put McSwan's body into a large metal drum in his basement and filled it with sulphuric acid. Haigh returned to the basement two days later and found almost all of the body had disintegrated. Only a bit of sludge was left in the bottom of the drum, which he dumped down a manhole.

Haigh then went to McSwan's parents and told them their son had gone to Scotland to avoid being drafted into the war. He then managed to talk his way into taking over McSwan's responsibilities of collecting the rent for his parents. Eventually, he even moved into McSwan's residence while collecting the rents, but he still kept his old place.

However, McSwan's parents started to become suspicious as the war was ending, and they still hadn't heard from their son. On July 2, 1945, Haigh invited McSwan's parents to come over to his place by telling them that their son was there and waiting to see them. Haigh killed them both by hitting them over the head with a pipe, and he disposed of their bodies the same way as he did their son. He sold the parents' properties, took the money, and moved into the Onslow Court Hotel in Kensington.

Haigh had a bad gambling problem, and within two years, he had gone through all of the money he stole from the McSwan family. He was almost broke again.

While living at the hotel, he met and became friends with many wealthy people. Archibald and Rose Henderson were two people he met, and they stayed at the hotel until their new home was purchased. They both knew that Haigh was a great piano player, so they asked him to come and play at their housewarming party in their new house. Haigh believed that he needed to get himself a gun to commit a robbery, so going to the Henderson house was the perfect opportunity. Sometime during the night, he snuck into their bedroom and stole their handgun from the bedside table.

On February 12, 1948, Haigh told Archibald about something he had invented and wanted him to see it. So he picked up Archibald, drove him to his apartment, took him into the basement, and shot him in the head with his gun. Haigh immediately returned to Henderson's home and told Rose that her husband had fallen ill, so she returned to his place with him. Once there, Haigh shot her in the head as well. He placed both bodies in drums full of sulphuric acid. He created a fraudulent document allowing him to sell their house and possession and collect the money.

Another person Haigh met and became friends with while living at the hotel was sixty-nine-year-old Olive Durand-Deacon, who had moved into the hotel after her lawyer husband died. She often talked about starting a business to make and sell artificial nails for women. One day, Haigh approached her and told her he was interested in helping her make the nails at his workshop. He invited her there to see it. She agreed to go with Haigh to see his workshop. On February 18, 1949, once he got her there, he shot her in the back of her head. But before placing her body into a drum of acid, he removed all of her valuables.

A few days after Olive failed to return to the hotel, the police were notified. After questioning guests at the hotel, they learned that she had been meeting with Haigh recently. Police ran a background check on Haigh and learned about his criminal history of fraud and robberies. Police arrested Haigh and brought him in for questioning.

Detectives searched Haigh's residence and workshop, finding several documents belonging to the Hendersons and McSwans. They also found a dry cleaning receipt for Olive's expensive coat. Police discovered part of a human foot, dentures belonging to Olive, and what turned out to be over twenty-eight pounds of human body fat. Haigh was dumping what was left of the bodies after they were dissolved in the acid on the land in the rear of his property.

Once confronted with all the evidence that investigators found, Haigh confessed to the murders he had committed. In all, there were a total of nine murders. Haigh believed that if the police couldn't find the bodies of his victims, he couldn't be found guilty of the murders.

Detectives were able to confirm six of the murders and charged him with six counts of premeditated murder. Haigh's defense was that he was insane. He even told the jury that he often drank the blood of his victims. He was found guilty on all six counts of murder and sentenced to death. On August 10, 1949, Haigh was hanged to death.

SEVEN

John Straffen

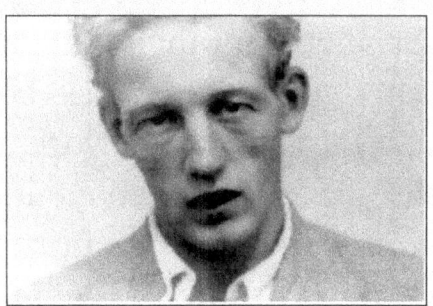

On February 27, 1930, John Thomas Straffen was born in Bordon Camp, Hampshire, England. His father was a British Army soldier stationed at the base where John and his two older siblings were born. When he turned two, his father was sent abroad to India, and the family went with him. In March 1938, when his father was discharged, they moved back to England, to Bath, Somerset.

Within the first year of living in Bath, Straffen began to get into trouble at school for stealing small items from other students. He then started skipping classes, and when an attendance officer caught him, he was sent to a guidance counselor to find out what was happening. Even with the attention, Straffen tried to steal a girl's purse, got caught, and was sent to juvenile court, where he was given two years of probation.

During this probation period, the officer reported to Straffen's mother that her son could not distinguish right from wrong. He also noted that she was so busy trying to work and keep the house that she did nothing about it. The officer then sent Straffen to a psychiatrist for analysis. The doctor certified Straffen as mentally defective with an IQ of only 58 and figured he had the mental age of a six-year-old even though he was ten years old at the time.

As a result of this diagnosis, Straffen was sent to a school for mentally defective children in Sambourne, Warwickshire, where he would have to live as well as study. He continued in school until he reached the age of sixteen in 1946. When he was finally released, he returned to his home in

Bath. At first, he worked a few temporary jobs until he found a full-time job at a clothing factory.

Straffen began to steal small items from people without being caught, but instead of bringing home the things he had taken, he would take them to abandoned homes and leave them there.

On July 27, 1947, the police were notified of an assault by the mother of a thirteen-year-old girl. The girl claimed that a young man named John had approached her and placed his hand over her mouth firmly, then asked her what she would do if he killed her and claimed that he had done it before. The incident was not connected to Straffen at the time.

About six weeks after that, Straffen had a quarrel with another girl, so he went to her house and strangled five of her family's chickens. Police arrested Straffen and brought him in for questioning. He happily confessed to killing the chickens as well as several other crimes he had done that police never associated him with. After an examination from a doctor, he was sent to the Hortham Colony in Bristol, where he was committed.

Hortham Colony was a transition establishment expressly set up to help mentally disturbed patients make the transition back into the community. Straffen did well there, and by July of 1949, he was transferred to a minimum security agricultural hostel in Winchester. But in February 1950, he was caught stealing a bag of walnuts and was returned to Hortham Colony. In August of that same year, Straffen got up one morning, left, and returned to his home. When police came to bring him back, he resisted and fought with them.

In 1951, Straffen was examined at a medical hospital in Briston, where they discovered he had suffered severe damage to his cerebral cortex when he was young. Doctors suspected that while Straffen was living in India as a young child, he probably suffered from an attack of encephalitis. With this being his only issue from the exam, he was now on unescorted day passes, allowing him to go home and stay. He was then allowed to work for an agricultural company and, on July 10, 1951, was given a release date of only six months out.

During one of his unescorted releases from Hortham, Straffen went to a movie theater to see a film. While walking to the theater, he passed five-year-old Brenda Goddard, collecting flowers from her family's front yard. He stopped and told her he knew a place with much prettier flowers and could take her there. The two walked a little way until they came to a fence. He lifted her over the wall where she fell on the other side. He followed her, and while they were behind the fence, he strangled her to death. Straffen hopped back over the wall and went to the theater as if nothing had happened, and he never tried to cover up the body. After police found the girl's body, they began to interview all criminals who were free in the area during that time. One of the people they questioned was Straffen on August 3rd, even though they didn't consider him violent.

Straffen's next free day was August 8th, when he decided to see another movie at the theater. This time, while on his way there, he met Cicely Batstone, who was nine years old, and offered to take her to a movie. The two went and saw a show, and afterward, they got on a bus, which took them to the outskirts of town. Once they were in a remote field, Straffen strangled Batstone and left her there.

But while Straffen was with the girl on the bus, he was recognized by a few people, including the wife of one of the police officers who had interviewed Straffen before. The following day, after she told her husband about seeing Straffen with a young girl, they went to where she saw them getting off the bus. After a short look around, they found the murdered child. Straffen was immediately arrested as a suspect in the crime.

While Straffen was being interviewed, he admitted to killing Cicely Batstone and that he had also done the same thing to the other little girl, Brenda Goddard.

Straffen was charged with the murders of both girls and stood trial on October 17, 1951. During the trial, one of the doctors who had examined Straffen told the court that he was not fit to stand trial because he was insane. The jury agreed with his assessment, and Straffen was transferred to Broadmoor Hospital, a criminal lunatic asylum.

The following year, on April 29, 1952, while Straffen was working as a cleaner at Broadmoor, he managed to climb over a ten-foot wall and escaped. A few hours later, he ran into five-year-old Linda Bowyer, who was riding her bike down the road. He strangled her to death and left her out in the open on the road, where he came across her. Later that night, police captured Straffen and took him back to Broadmoor.

The following day, after the news broke about Bowyer being murdered, investigators went directly to the hospital and questioned Straffen.

He responded that he did not kill the girl on her bicycle. But they arrested and charged him with her murder. Since he was able to escape from Broadmoor, they transferred him to a more secure prison in Brixton.

In the Summer of 1952, Straffen was tried for the murder of Bowyer, where he pleaded insanity again. This time, the jury would not agree and convicted him of murder. He was sentenced to death. He appealed to the court, but the appeal was dismissed.

On August 29th, the Home Secretary announced that he recommended Straffen be reprieved and placed in prison for the rest of his life. Straffen died on November 19, 2007, while serving out his sentence in HM Prison Frankland in County Durham.

EIGHT

Donald Neilson

THE BLACK PANTHER

On August 1, 1936, Donald Neilson, born Donald Nappey, was born in Bradford, West Riding of Yorkshire, England. When he turned ten years old, his mother died from breast cancer. Throughout his childhood, Donald was constantly getting into trouble, fighting or stealing things, and he would always get talked to or warned by police because he was young.

When Neilson turned eighteen in 1955, he married Irene Tate, who was twenty years old. Three years into their marriage, he joined the British Army and was stationed in Kenya and Cyprus before returning home in the Fall of 1959.

The couple had a daughter, Kathryn, in 1960. Around this time, Donald legally changed his family name from Nappey to Neilson, mainly because of the teasing and bullying throughout school and while in the army. He didn't want the same thing to happen to his daughter.

Donald never had any past relatives with the Neilson name, but for some reason, it's the name he chose. A couple of theories about why "Neilson" came from his friends. In a BBC interview, Lena Fearnley, a friend who lived with the Neilson family for a short time, said that he took the name from the brand of ice cream they used to buy from the local ice cream man, called "Lord Neilson." Whereas two of Donald's friends, David Bell and Harry Hawkes, claimed that Donald had once bought a taxicab company that consisted of only one taxicab from a man named Neilson. Neither of these theories were ever confirmed.

In the first years of his criminal activity, Neilson committed over four hundred robberies and home thefts without being noticed by police. He usually didn't make much money from these small thefts, so he decided to get a gun to rob some smaller businesses. During one of his break-ins of a house in Cheshire, he found a handgun with some ammunition, so he took it.

The word about the home break-ins began to get out to the media, and soon, the newspapers started labeling Neilson as "The Phantom" and "Handy Andy." Once he heard that his crimes were making the news, he wanted to try to make each robbery look like different robbers had done it. So, he would steal a specific item, such as a clock, for four or five home robberies. And once that became the theme of the robberies, he would change and steal another particular item.

Now that he had a gun, he no longer had to waste his time committing many small house robberies. He could now move up to robbing places with more money and valuables. Between 1971 and 1974, Neilson robbed eighteen post offices.

In 1972, these robberies started to take on a violent nature as Neilson began to feel braver now that he had a weapon. He believed he could commit the robbery while people were still at the post office and no longer needed to hide. The first known assault was at a small post office, which was attached to the home of the postmaster, Leslie Richardson, and his wife. Once Richardson woke after hearing an intruder, he went to see what was going on. Neilson attacked him, and the two struggled. Richardson pulled off Neilson's mask and saw who he was. Neilson then stomped on Richardson's feet so hard that he broke several of his toes, then fled the scene. It was the police's first eyewitness description of the thief.

Two years later, in 1974, the post office robberies that Neilson had been committing started to become deadly. He shot three post office managers to death: in February, Donald Skepper in North Yorkshire, in September Derek Astin in Lancashire, and Sidney Grayland in West Midlands. During an interview with Astin's wife on television, she described the killer as very fast, like a panther, and wearing all-black clothing. The description led to Neilson's nickname changing to "The Black Panther."

On January 14, 1975, Neilson broke into the

home of famous business owner George Wittle, who he had been following through the newspapers for a few years. He thought that he could make a lot of money by kidnapping and holding Wittle's daughter, Lesley, for ransom. Before Neilson took off with Lesley, he left a note asking for fifty thousand pounds and saying he would get his daughter back home safely.

After the police and George Wittle's brother made a few mistakes, like not dropping the ransom money at the correct location and time, Lesley was found hanging from a wire in the bottom of a sewer on March 7, 1975. She had died from the shock of a fall, which made her heart stop.

Tony White and Stuart Mackenzie, two on-duty police officers, were sitting in their police car one night in December 1975 in North Nottinghamshire, keeping an eye on traffic, when they spotted a suspicious-looking man, Neilson, walking on the side of the road carrying a duffle bag. As he walked by the officers, he turned his head away from them. Mackenzie shouted at the man and asked him to come to the car.

When he approached the officers, he pulled a shotgun out of his bag and ordered White to get into the back seat of the vehicle. Neilson jumped into the passenger seat, pointed the gun at Mackenzie's side, and ordered him to drive.

As they drove along, Neilson asked the officers if they had any rope in the backseat. White pretended to be looking on the floor. At the same time, Neilson kept his eye on him when, suddenly, Mackenzie slammed on the brakes, causing the gun to go off. Mackenzie jumped out of the car and ran to a nearby fish and chip shop. Roy Morris and Keith Wood ran from the restaurant and helped the officers subdue and arrest Neilson.

During his interrogation, Neilson admitted to having kidnapped Lesley Whittle, and his fingerprints were a match to the ones they found at the crime scene. Neilson's defense attorney would later claim that Whittle had accidentally fallen, and that was why she died.

Neilson was charged and tried for the kidnapping and murder of Lesley Whittle in July 1976. He was found guilty and given a sentence of life imprisonment. Three weeks later, he stood trial for the murder of the three postmasters. He was also convicted and given life sentences for each of those crimes. Neilson also received an additional sixty years for the other charges of kidnapping, blackmail, and burglary.

Neilson's wife, Irene, was also arrested for cashing over eighty money orders that her husband had stolen from the post offices that he robbed. She was later convicted on all counts. Irene claimed that her husband forced her to cash the money orders. She was first given three years probation for her crimes, but the light sentence wasn't good enough for those living in the area. They demanded a more severe punishment to be given to her. Upon review of the sentence, she was given a one-year sentence in prison.

Donald Neilson died on December 18, 2011, after being taken from the prison to the hospital the previous day with breathing difficulties.

NINE

Patrick Mackay

THE DEVIL'S DISCIPLE

On September 25, 1952, Patrick Mackay, a.k.a. David Groves, was born the oldest of three children in Middlesex, London, England. His father was a Scottish accountant, and his mother was from Guyana. Mackay was constantly in trouble with his father and, at times, hurt or beaten. When he went to school, he would do the same to his classmates, often bullying them for no real reason. He wasn't a good student either, and whenever his teacher would try to get him to pay attention in class or do his homework, he would make a scene and start yelling and calling them names. His classmates and teachers also disclosed that Mackay was cruel to small animals – he used to find a bird and rip its wings off in front of them.

In 1962, Mackay's father died of a heart attack while he was driving to work. Patrick refused to accept it and refused to go to the funeral in Scotland with his family. He started carrying a photo of his father and continued telling everyone he met that his father was still alive.

Around the house, Mackay took over as the "man of the family." He began hitting his sisters anytime he felt they did something wrong. His attacks soon were aimed towards his mother, and he began to hit her whenever she didn't do something that he asked her to. The police were called to the home at least four times a week because of the yelling and screaming from their fights. The beatings became so loud the neighbors would ultimately call the police.

When Mackay turned fifteen, he was sent to a

psychiatrist to be analyzed. He was officially diagnosed as a psychopath. Between then and the time he turned twenty-one, he was physically removed from the home eighteen times and placed in different institutions. He would usually remain in one of these institutions anywhere from three days to a month. His longest stay was from 1968 to 1972 at the Moss Side School in Liverpool.

After he was released from the last institution in 1972, he moved into a small apartment in London. He became obsessed with Nazism to the point where he changed his name to "Franklin Bollvolt the First" and covered all of his walls with swastikas and other nazi memorabilia.

Mackay began committing petty thefts in the wealthier parts of London, including muggings, grab and runs from expensive shops, and dining and dashing in finer restaurants. Then, he started focusing on older women to steal from. He would start a conversation with them and befriend them, and once he gained their trust enough to get invited to their home, he would steal from them.

One such victim was Isabella Griffith, an eighty-four-year-old who lived in Chelsea, London. On February 24, 1974, Mackay gained an invite to her home. Once inside, he beat her up and strangled her to death. Then he stole all the money and valuables he could find.

His next victim was Adele Price, another older woman who lived in Chelsea. Mackay got into her home on March 10, 1975, by asking her for a drink of water. Once inside, he also beat and strangled his victim and then stole her money. As he was leaving the property, Mackay passed Price's granddaughter, who was visiting at the time. Unbeknownst to her, she had just passed her grandmother's killer.

Less than two weeks later, Mackay entered the home of Father Anthony Crean on March 21, 1975, and brutally murdered him with an axe. Again, he stole anything of value and left the murder weapon at the scene. While leaving, he was seen by many people who gave the police a good description of the assailant.

During the investigation, one of the detectives assigned to the Crean murder case was also the same officer called to a prior incident involving the priest and Mackay. Apparently, Mackay had broken into Crean's house before, stealing one of his checks for thirty pounds. After he was arrested for that crime, Mackay was convicted and ordered to pay a fine.

Given the history, the police picked up

Mackay and brought him for questioning about the murder. They took Mackay's fingerprints and also searched his apartment. His fingerprints ended up matching fingerprints found at the crime scene and other crime scenes as well. Furthermore, several pieces of stolen jewelry were found at his apartment.

During Mackay's interviews with the police, he confessed to having murdered Crean, Isabella Griffiths, and Adele Price, and according to him, that was all he was responsible for.

Police placed him in a cell with an informant to see if they could learn anything more from him. While in the cell, he told the informant about at least six other murders he had committed. Detectives then looked into the murders he talked about. They compared the descriptions and locations of those murders to the unsolved murders in the area. They were able to find several matches.

The first murder police were able to connect was of Heidi Mnilk, a seventeen-year-old German girl who had been working as a live-in babysitter for a family in London. While traveling on a train, Heidi had been stabbed and thrown off near Catford. The second murder police were able to connect was Mary Hynes, who was stabbed to death and robbed in Kentish Town on July 20, 1973. Police were also able to confirm a homeless man who was murdered and thrown off a bridge into the Thames River in January 1974. The fourth and fifth murders were Stephanie Britton, a fifty-seven-year-old grandmother, and her four-year-old grandson, Christopher Martin, who she was babysitting at the time. He strangled both of them to death and stole her money. The sixth connected murder was that of Frank Goodman on June 13, 1974. Mackay killed him with a metal pipe to take his pack of cigarettes from him. The seventh murder he told his cellmate about was that of ninety-two-year-old Sarah Rodmell in Hackney. Mackay eventually admitted to the murder and told officers what happened. On December 23, 1974, when he entered Sarah's home, he suffocated her by putting a sock in her mouth.

Even though he admitted to Sarah's murder, it was challenging for the police to prove the other six murders if Mackay wouldn't officially confess to them. No physical evidence was left at the scenes to connect him to the crimes.

In November 1975, Mackay was brought to trial, where he was found guilty of manslaughter for the three murders of Adele Price, Anthony

Crean, and Isabella Griffith, but only because he pleaded guilty due to diminished capacity. Mackay was sentenced to a minimum of twenty years in prison.

Even though his defense lawyers wanted him to be placed in a hospital, the court found him sane, asserting his psychopathy was a personality disorder and not a mental disorder.

Mackay has been up for release on parole a few times but has always been denied. He is considered by many to be the most prolific serial killer in the United Kingdom. Even though he was sentenced to twenty years, he remains in prison today. As of 2024, he has served more than forty-eight years so far.

TEN

Kenneth Erskine

STOCKWELL STRANGLER

K enneth Erskine was born in Hammersmith, London, England, on July 1, 1963. He was one of four boys his Antiguan father and British mother abandoned, and they attended various schools. By the age of twelve, Erskine started getting into trouble, once even trying to drown a classmate during a field trip. He continued his violent streak throughout school until he quit.

After leaving school, Erskine moved from place to place, never really having a home. He usually broke into homes owned by older people and stole items he could sell quickly. On April 9, 1986, Erskine broke into seventy-eight-year-old Nancy Emms' home in Wandsworth. He smothered her to death with a pillow and left, taking her TV. When her body was discovered, they initially thought she died in her sleep until her nurse arrived and noticed that her television was missing. The post-mortem exam established that not only had she died from strangulation, but she had also been sexually assaulted.

On June 8th, sixty-seven-year-old Janet Cockett's body was found in her apartment. The family member who found her believed that she had died in her sleep of natural causes. But again, the post-morten exam showed that she had been strangled to death. In her case, she had not been raped. Police were able to get a palm print from outside her window that possibly belonged to the killer. Erskine broke into another apartment in

Cockett's building on that same date. It belonged to an older man who lived alone, but when Erskine heard people outside the man's door, he fled out the window and ran before he had a chance to assault the man or take anything.

Erskine then went to a nursing home located in Stockwell on June 28th. He broke into two units that night. His first victim was an eighty-four-year-old Valentine Gleim, and his second was ninety-four-year-old Zbigniew Strabawa. In both cases, he sexually assaulted the men and stole their valuable items.

Just over a week later, on July 8th, Erskine attacked another man, eighty-four-year-old William Carman, in his home in Islington. He sexually assaulted Carman, then strangled him and took the small amount of cash the man had in his apartment before fleeing. The same day, Erskine returned to the nursing home in Stockwell and broke into another apartment there belonging to seventy-four-year-old William Downes, where he again sexually assaulted the man, then strangled him to death before fleeing with his money.

Erskine's final known victim was eighty-three-year-old Florence Tisdall, who lived by herself in the Ranelagh Gardens Mansion in Fulham. She was found dead in her apartment by the building manager on July 23rd. The post-mortem showed that she had been sexually assaulted and strangled to death.

Police had Erskine on their suspect list because of his previous convictions of burglary and assaults, but they were unable to find him to bring him in for questioning. He was finally arrested on July 28th at the Social Security office.

Police then matched Erskine's palm print to the palm print they had lifted from the window at the Cockett crime scene. They called in the only surviving victim of Erskine, seventy-four-year-old Fred Prentice, whom Erskine assaulted in his apartment the month before. Prentice was able to identify that Erskine was his attacker that night.

Erskine stood trial in January 1987 and was convicted of seven murders. He was sentenced to life imprisonment with a minimum of forty years to be served before a chance of parole. After the court determined that he had a mental disorder, he was transferred from prison and placed in Broadmoor Hospital, where he remains today.

In 2006, a mental assessment of Erskine determined that he was a chronic schizophrenic and had an antisocial personality disorder. Erskine used those results to file an appeal of his conviction in 2009. The Appeal Court lowered his murder conviction to manslaughter because of his diminished responsibility.

ELEVEN

Bruce George Peter Lee

Bruce George Peter Lee, born Peter George Dinsdale, was born in Manchester, England, on July 31, 1960, and was raised in a children's home. His mother was a prostitute, and she couldn't handle his epilepsy or his spastic right arm and leg. He walked with a limp and carried his right arm on his chest. Everyone throughout town used the nickname "Daft Peter" when talking about him.

When Peter turned nineteen, he got a job doing labor for a construction company. His mother married a man whose last name was Lee, and because he was fascinated with Bruce Lee, he changed his first name to Bruce and took his new stepfather's last name, Lee. So he could now go by the name Bruce Lee.

On December 4, 1979, a fire suddenly broke out at Edith Hastie's house on Selby Street in Yorkshire. Edith Hastie and her four sons, Charles, fifteen; Paul, twelve; Thomas, nine; and Peter, eight, were inside. Charles was able to help his mother escape by pushing her from her bedroom window but could not help his brothers. Opening the window fed the fire, which badly burned Charles and his two brothers.

They were all taken to the hospital, but Charles died that same night. Two days later, Peter died from his wounds, and about two weeks later, Paul also succumbed to his injuries. Thomas, who had muscle dystrophy, survived by escaping through a window in the back of the house where the flames were less intense. But he still needed treatment for his burns. Hastie also had three daughters staying with relatives that night, so they were unharmed. Hastie's husband, the father of her children, was in prison during the time of the fire.

The police began their investigation of the fire, and when they started to canvass the neighborhood, they learned that the Hastie family was not liked very much. They were often considered a problem, and most neighbors wished the Hasties would move. But what shocked the police most was the fact that nobody seemed to care about the children being burned to death in the fire, and almost none of them even went to their funeral.

It was revealed that the Hastie children often stole things from their neighbors, fought with them, called them names, and, in some cases, damaged the neighbor's property. Police figured this could be the possible motivation behind the burning of their home. They began to question other kids living in the neighborhood, including Lee.

Later, during Lee's questioning, he eventually admitted to pouring paraffin into Hastie's mailbox and setting it on fire. He claimed he had only done this because Charles had been blackmailing him. It seemed the two were having a sexual relationship, and Charles threatened that he would go to the police and tell them unless Lee gave him some money. Since Charles was only fifteen, and Lee was now ninety, it was sexually assaulting a minor. Lee admitted to starting the fire because he was mad at Charles, but he said he had no intention of killing anyone.

During Lee's conversations with the detectives, he accidentally admitted to starting nine other fires in town over the previous seven years. When police reviewed each of these fires, they realized that a total of twenty-six people had died from these fires, including a six-month-old baby.

Lee claimed that he started these fires randomly and for no reason. He said that, in most cases, he didn't even know who lived in the houses he burned. He contended that the only fire he planned was the Hastie's home fire.

Detectives then took Lee around the city, asking him to show them where each fire he lit was. He couldn't give the exact dates he burned each place, but he could describe where and how he lit the fires, and they all matched the evidence.

Lee was charged with twenty-six counts of murder, and his trial began on January 20, 1981. It was held at the Leeds Crown Court. He pleaded not guilty to all counts. But he did admit to committing twenty six counts of manslaughter on the grounds of having diminished responsibility. He also admitted to the eleven counts of arson. The prosecutors accepted his pleas rather than go through an expensive and lengthy trial.

After a public inquiry into the fire at the Wensley Lodge, the criminal cases review board decided that the fire was accidental and that Lee couldn't be held responsible for the fire or deaths involved in that case. This finding allowed his defense to appeal his conviction and have eleven of the manslaughter convictions dismissed. Lee also recanted his confession when he heard about the ruling of the commission board.

Lee brought forward another appeal in 2021, saying that because of his physical handicaps, he could not have committed some of the fires that he had confessed to earlier, claiming that he only admitted because of his limited mental capacity. The Court of Appeal agreed with Lee on two of the arson cases and acquitted him on both, which also released him from responsibility for three of his manslaughter convictions.

TWELVE

Steven Grieveson

THE SUNDERLAND STRANGLER

S teven John Grieveson was born in England on December 14, 1970. He gained infamy as "The Sunderland Strangler," a British serial killer responsible for the deaths of four teenage boys in Sunderland, England, between

1990 and 1994. Grieveson earned the nickname because of the location of his crimes and his preferred method of murder, which involved ligature strangulation. He was convicted of three murders at Leeds Crown Court on February 28, 1996, receiving three life sentences, with a minimum of 35 years recommended before any consideration for release by the Home Secretary. Later, in October 2013, Grieveson faced yet another conviction, this time for the 1990 murder of 14-year-old Simon Martin at Newcastle Crown Court, which resulted in a fourth life sentence. He is currently serving his sentences at HMP Full Sutton, a maximum-security prison in the East Riding of Yorkshire, England.

On November 26, 1993, Grieveson murdered eighteen-year-old Thomas Kelly in an abandoned Fulwell allotment shed in Sunderland. Kelly's body was then set ablaze. Later, on February 4, 1994, Grieveson murdered fifteen-year-old David Hanson on Roker Terrace. Then, on February 25, 1994, he took the life of another fifteen-year-old, David Grieff, in a deserted allotment just 50 yards away from where Thomas Kelly had been killed three months earlier.

All three victims were either current or former students of Monkwearmouth Academy. There was speculation among law enforcement, school staff, and fellow students that the victims had known their assailant. It was possible that Grieveson had ties to Monkwearmouth Academy or attended there at some point. Grieveson attended Hylton Red House School at the time of the murders.

Initially, Grieveson was arrested on March 11, 1994, for an attempted burglary at the residence on Roker Terrace, where David Hanson's charred remains had been discovered. Later, in November 1995, he was charged with the three murders following an extensive investigation.

In 1996, he went on trial for the three murders and six weeks later was sentenced to three life terms, with a minimum of 35 years in prison. During the trial, held at Leeds Crown Court, it was established that Grieveson had killed the three boys to conceal evidence of his homosexuality. Thomas Kelly's father expressed relief at Grieveson's conviction: "It is a great relief this monster is off the streets so no other family.

While serving his three life sentences at Full

Sutton Prison, Grieveson was questioned, and even arrested, regarding the May 1990 murder of fourteen-year-old Simon Martin at Gilside House in Roker in November 2000. However, he was not charged at the time.

In June 2004, Grieveson wrote a letter to the Victim Liaison Services where he confessed to the killings of the three victims from 1993 and 1994 but omitted any mention of his involvement in Simon Martin's murder. Therefore, he still wasn't officially charged for Martin's death.

However, that changed on November 22, 2012, when Grieveson was formally charged with Simon Martin's murder. He broke down and admitted responsibility for Martin's demise on February 11, 2013, but claimed there was no premeditation in the murder. Following a trial at Newcastle Crown Court, he was found guilty of Simon Martin's murder in October 2013.

On February 20, 2014, Grieveson faced yet another arrest after suspicion landed on him for the 1992 murder of a seven-year-old girl named Nikki Allan. Her lifeless body was discovered with stab wounds in a deserted warehouse back in October 1992. The neighbor who had initially confessed to the crime was acquitted two years later due to concerns regarding the police's interrogation methods. Although the victim in this case was female and she had succumbed to stab wounds, the severe blunt force trauma to her head bore a resemblance to injuries inflicted on Simon Martin.

While Grieveson was questioned about possible involvement, detectives later announced no immediate action against him in connection to their ongoing investigation into Allan's murder. Then, in 2017, a breakthrough occurred when authorities revealed they had obtained a complete DNA profile of Allan's assailant from prior evidence. In 2019, DNA findings led to the re-arrest of a previous suspect. It turned out that it was not Grieveson but fifty-five-year-old David Boyd who murdered Nikki Allan. He was convicted of her murder in May 2023. Boyd, a known child molester, had a connection to the victim's family, as his partner had served as Allan's babysitter in the early 1990s.

THIRTEEN

Beverly Allitt

ANGEL OF DEATH

Beverley Gail Allitt, a.k.a. "Angel of Death," is a British serial killer convicted of murdering four babies, attempting to murder three others, and causing grievous bodily harm to six more at Grantham and Kesteven Hospital in Lincolnshire between February and April 1991. At the time, she worked as a State Enrolled Nurse in the hospital's children's ward. Allitt administered large doses of insulin to at least two victims, while another victim was found with a significant air bubble in their body. She was ultimately sentenced to thirteen life terms in 1993.

Born on October 4, 1968, Beverly Gail Allitt spent her childhood in the village of Corby Glen, near Grantham. She grew up with two sisters and a brother. Her father, Richard, worked in a liquor store, while her mother worked as a school cleaner. Allitt attended Charles Read Secondary Modern School after failing the Kesteven and Grantham Girls' School entrance exams. Like many teenage girls, she frequently volunteered for babysitting roles. At age sixteen, she left school and pursued a nursing course at Grantham College.

When so many babies started dying of cardiac arrest in such a short period, suspicion arose among medical staff. After the fourth death, that of Becky Phillips, the police were brought in to investigate. Their investigation revealed that Nurse Beverly Allitt was the only nurse present during all the incidents and the only one who had access to the drugs used.

Allitt pleaded not guilty to all charges, which

included four counts of murder, eleven counts of attempted murder, and eleven counts of assault causing grievous bodily harm. On May 28, 1993, she was found guilty on all counts and received thirteen concurrent life sentences.

Although initially sent to prison after her conviction, Allitt is currently serving her time at Rampton Secure Hospital in Nottinghamshire. In the documentary *Trevor McDonald and the Killer Nurse*, which aired in 2018, Allitt allegedly didn't think she would be sent to prison. After she was sent there, she went on a hunger strike. After a week of refusing to eat or drink anything, she was transferred to Rampton Secure Hospital, despite two leading psychologists, upon examination, concluding that she was mentally sane and should be in prison.

It was reported that Allitt admitted to all thirteen attacks in an application to stay at the hospital and not ever be sent back to prison. None of the families of her victims were informed of her confession.

On December 6, 2007, Justice Stanley Burnton ordered her to serve the original minimum sentence of thirty years, which expired in November 2021. His order renders her eligible for parole. However, her release remains uncertain. Justice David Latham, the sentencing judge, described her as "a danger" to society and deemed her unlikely ever to be considered safe for release.

The motives behind Allitt's actions remain unclear. It is unknown exactly why Allitt perpetrated the attacks on thirteen children during that fateful fifty-nine days in 1991. One theory suggests symptoms of a factitious disorder, also known as Munchausen syndrome by proxy, wherein a perpetrator fabricates or induces illnesses in someone under their care to gain attention for themselves.

On October 3, 2023, reports emerged of Allitt appearing before a mental health tribunal for potential transfer to a mainstream prison. If approved, she could be eligible for parole after six months.

FOURTEEN

Colin Ireland

GAY SLAYER

Colin Ireland was a British serial killer notorious as the "Gay Slayer" due to his targeting of gay victims. According to criminologist David Wilson, Ireland exhibited psychopathic traits after growing up in a severely dysfunctional environment. He began his criminal activities at the age of sixteen, leading to stints in borstals (youth detention centers) and prisons. While residing in Southend, Ireland frequented the Coleherne, a gay pub in Earl's Court, London. He specifically targeted men who favored submissive roles and engaged in sadomasochistic activities, using their initial consent as a guise for his sinister intentions.

Despite claiming heterosexuality and being twice married to women, Ireland feigned homosexuality to gain the trust of potential victims. He contended that sexual motives did not drive his killings. He was highly organized and meticulously planned each murder, carrying a complete kit of tools, including rope, handcuffs, and a change of clothes. After committing the murders, he cleansed the crime scene of any incriminating evidence and remained until morning to avoid raising suspicions by leaving at night.

Ireland was ultimately convicted of five counts of murder on December 20, 1993, receiving multiple life sentences. He remained incarcerated until his death on February 21, 2012, at the age of 57.

Born on March 16, 1954, in Dartford, Kent, Colin Ireland entered the world to an unmarried teenage couple. Shortly after his birth, his father departed, leaving him and his seventeen-year-old mother behind. Without his father's presence, Ireland's birth certificate remained void of his father's name, and he remained unaware of his identity. Raised in impoverished circumstances by his mother, the pair endured frequent relocations. In the early 1960s, his mother remarried, leading to Ireland's temporary placement in care when she became pregnant. He reunited with his mother, who married another man in 1966.

During their time in Sheerness, Kent, Ireland encountered unsettling experiences, including being approached by men with inappropriate intentions on multiple occasions and being subjected to voyeurism by individuals with predatory tendencies. As he entered his mid-teens, his life took a darker turn, resulting in his incarceration in a youth detention facility for theft. While there, he deliberately ignited another resident's possessions. At the age of seventeen, Ireland faced a robbery conviction, culminating in an escape and subsequent return to the borstal.

As Ireland got older, he struggled to make ends meet. He took on various manual labor jobs.

In December 1975, his life took a darker turn when he was convicted of car theft, criminal damage, and two burglaries, resulting in an eighteen-month prison sentence.

Upon release in November 1976, he relocated to Swindon, Wiltshire, briefly residing with a woman and her children. But his criminal activities persisted, leading to a conviction for extortion in 1977 and resulting in another eighteen-month prison term. In 1980, Ireland faced a robbery conviction, serving a two-year sentence, followed by another conviction for attempted deception in 1981.

In 1982, Ireland married Virginia Zammit. The couple and their daughter settled in London's Holloway area. However, marital discord ensued, culminating in a divorce in 1987 after Ireland's infidelity came to light.

In 1989, he wed Janet Young in Devon, where his violent behavior and theft strained their relationship. By the early 1990s, they separated, leaving Young and her children homeless.

Ireland relocated to Southend-on-Sea, where he experienced homelessness himself before securing accommodation in a hostel. It was during this time that he encountered the Coleherne

Arms, a gay pub in Earl's Court, London, where he would later target his victims.

Peter Walker, a forty-five-year-old choreographer, invited Ireland to his flat in Battersea. Once there, Walker was restrained and suffocated with a plastic bag placed over his head by Ireland. As a macabre gesture, Ireland arranged two teddy bears in a suggestive position on the victim's body, leaving Walker's dogs confined in another room.

The following day, with no reports of the crime in the media, Ireland contacted the Samaritans (an emotional support organization) and a journalist from *The Sun* newspaper, revealing details of the dogs and confessing to the murder. He even expressed a desire for notoriety as a serial killer. Later, a former boyfriend of Walker informed the police that Walker did not usually engage in sadomasochism and that it was likely Ireland coerced him.

Christopher Dunn, a thirty-seven-year-old librarian residing in Wealdstone, was discovered naked and wearing only a harness. Initially, his demise was thought to be the result of an accident during an erotic encounter. Given his residence was a separate district from Walker's, a different team of investigators handled the case.

Consequently, the connection between Dunn's death and Walker's was not immediately established.

Thirty-five-year-old businessman Perry Bradley III was at the Coleherne Pub drinking the night he met Ireland. Bradley was the son of Perry Bradley Jr., the fundraiser for the Texas Democratic Party. The two men hit it off at the pub and decided to return to Bradley's place. Once they got there, the two started to become intimate. Ireland told Bradley that he couldn't get aroused unless there was some bondage going on and asked if he could tie Bradley up. But he wasn't fussy about the idea. Eventually, Bradley would agree, though, to let Ireland tie him up.

After Ireland got Bradley tied up face down on his bed, including having a noose around his neck, he asked for money as well as the PIN for his bank card. Once Ireland got the PIN, he told Bradley to go to sleep and that he would leave. Once Bradley was asleep, Ireland decided to use the noose to strangle him to death before leaving, as he knew that Bradley could identify him. Before leaving Bradley's place, he placed a doll on his head. After Bradley died, Ireland went to the bank, taking 200 pounds out of his account.

Ireland began to get upset because after murdering three, he wasn't getting any media attention. He decided that he would kill again within three days. It wasn't long before he met Andrew Collier, a thirty-three-year-old apartment building manager. After they had a dinner date, Collier invited him over for a drink at his house in Dalston. A loud crash occurred outside shortly after the two were in the house, so they went to the front room to see what caused the noise. While Ireland looked out the window, he inadvertently put his hands on the window cell and left his fingerprints there, which the police were able to find later.

When the two men became intimate and ended up on Collier's bed, Ireland demanded Collier give him his bank card and PIN. When Collier refused, he strangled him to death. Ireland then killed Collier's cat and, after putting a condom on Collier's penis, he put the dead cat's mouth over it. Later, Ireland claimed that he only did this because when looking through Collier's drawers, looking for his banking card and anything he could find, he located a blood test confirming that Collier was HIV positive, which made him angry. After the murder, Ireland phoned the police, asking them why they had not connected the murders. He left Collier's house after finding only seventy pounds in cash.

Ireland's next victim was Emanuel Spiteri, a forty-one-year-old Maltese chef he encountered at the Coleherne pub. Spiteri agreed to be restrained and was, after that, bound to his bed by Ireland. Despite demands, Spiteri refused to provide his PIN. Ireland proceeded to strangle him with a noose, as he had done with previous victims.

After finishing his usual post-murder cleanup, Ireland set fire to the flat before departing. However, the fire caused only minor damage. Later, he phoned the police to inform them of a body at the scene of the fire, adding that he had no plans to kill again.

There were allegations suggesting that the initial police response to the murders may have been hindered by homophobia. It would explain the delay in linking all the killings. It took a long time; however, police eventually established connections between all five murders. The media covered the crimes extensively, leading to widespread awareness within the gay community of a serial killer targeting gay men.

Investigations uncovered that Spiteri had left the Coleherne pub with his assailant and traveled home by train. Surveillance footage from Charing

Cross Station captured the pair and provided crucial evidence. Recognizing himself in the footage, Ireland voluntarily approached the police, claiming to be the man seen with Spiteri but denying involvement in the murder. He alleged he left Spiteri with another individual at the flat. Nevertheless, police discovered fingerprints in Collier's flat, which they linked to Ireland.

Ireland was charged for the murders of Collier and Spiteri. While awaiting trial in prison, he confessed to the other three killings. He explained to the police that his targeting of gay men wasn't driven by personal animosity but rather by their perceived vulnerability. He admitted to adopting a pretense of being gay to lure his victims. His motive for robbery stemmed from his unemployment at the time, and his need for funds to and from London while seeking victims.

Ireland's trial was at the Old Bailey on December 20, 1993. He pleaded guilty to all charges and received life sentences for each. Justice Sachs described him as "exceptionally frightening and dangerous," condemning his actions as "carnage" for taking five lives.

The tabloid press sensationalized Ireland's crimes, dubbing him "The Gay Slayer" and "Jack The Gripper," as highlighted by the *News of the*

World. On December 22, 2006, Ireland was among thirty-five life-sentence prisoners identified by the Home Office, indicating they were unlikely ever to be released.

On February 21, 2012, Ireland died while still an inmate at Wakefield Prison. A spokesperson for Her Majesty's Prison Service stated, "His death is believed to have resulted from natural causes, pending a post-mortem examination." Subsequent investigation revealed that pulmonary fibrosis and a previously sustained fractured hip earlier in the month were identified as primary factors contributing to his demise.

FIFTEEN

Levi Bellfield

THE BUS STOP KILLER

L evi Bellfield, originally born Levi Rabbetts on May 17, 1968, in Isleworth, London, England, is notorious in English criminal history. He is characterized as a serial killer, sex offender, rapist, kidnapper, and burglar. The severity of his crimes led to the imposition of a whole life order by the judge, ensuring he would spend the rest of his life behind bars without the possibility of parole. Levi Bellfield holds the dubious distinction of being the first individual in history to receive two such orders.

Detective Chief Inspector Colin Sutton, who spearheaded the initial murder investigation, offered insight into Bellfield's persona. Despite initially presenting himself as pleasant and cheerful, Bellfield revealed a darker side—cunning, violent, and capable of swift shifts from charm to malice.

Bellfield's modus operandi involved preying on familiar streets, targeting victims he knew intimately. Ex-girlfriends recounted a chilling pattern: initial charm giving way to complete control and malevolence. Detective Sergeant Jo Brunt highlighted the recurring theme: Bellfield's charming facade masking a sinister and controlling nature. He said that Bellfield exuded a sense of entitlement and superiority when he operated a wheel-clamping business in his West Drayton neighborhood. His inflated ego drove him to assert dominance, particularly over young women who rebuffed his advances. The case of

Kate Sheedy illustrates this disturbing dynamic, where rejection swiftly escalated to violence.

Under police surveillance, Bellfield prowled the streets in his van, engaging with young girls at bus stops. CCTV footage captured Amélie Delagrange's last moments before her tragic encounter with Bellfield. She unwittingly crossed paths with him moments before becoming his victim.

The culmination of Bellfield's reign of terror came with his arrest on November 22, 2004, initially on suspicion of Amélie Delagrange's murder. Still, subsequent charges followed, including multiple counts of rape and assault dating back many years.

Bellfield's upbringing sheds some light on the factors contributing to his criminal behavior. Born to Jean Rabbetts and Joseph Bellfield, of Romani descent, he faced early tragedy with the death of his father from leukemia when he was just ten years old.

Raised alongside his four siblings on a Southwest London council estate, his childhood was marked by hardship. He attended several schools, including Forge Lane Junior School, Rectory Secondary School, and Feltham Comprehensive.

Levi's first brush with the law was when he was caught committing a burglary in 1981. He served no jail time since he was only thirteen and still a child. Over the years, his rap sheet expanded, including a 1990 conviction for assaulting a police officer, as well as various offenses related to theft and driving. By 2002, he had amassed nine convictions and almost a year behind bars.

Murders & Attacks

Amanda Jane "Milly" Dowler, a thirteen-year-old girl, vanished after leaving Walton-on-Thames Railway Station on March 21, 2002. Tragically, her body was discovered six months later in Yateley Heath Woods. In August 2009, Surrey Police compiled evidence implicating Bellfield in Dowler's murder, submitting it to the Crown Prosecution Service (CPS).

Marsha Louise McDonnell, aged nineteen, suffered a fatal attack near her home in Hampton on February 4, 2003. Struck over the head shortly after disembarking from the 111 bus from Kingston upon Thames, McDonnell succumbed to her injuries two days later. Bellfield's actions raised suspicions when he swiftly sold his Vauxhall Corsa, purchased just months before the murder, for a fraction of its value.

On May 28, 2004, eighteen-year-old **Kate Sheedy** was deliberately struck by a vehicle as she crossed a road near an industrial estate in Isleworth. Though she survived, sustaining multiple injuries, she spent weeks in hospital. Nearly four years later, Sheedy testified against Bellfield, providing crucial evidence that matched his description and vehicle at the time of the attack.

Amélie Delagrange, a twenty-two-year-old French student, met a tragic fate on Twickenham Green on August 19, 2004. Found with severe head injuries, she passed away in hospital the same night. Police quickly linked her death to McDonnell's, with Bellfield reportedly confessing to Delagrange's murder while in custody.

On March 2, 2006, he faced charges for Delagrange's murder, alongside attempted murder charges involving Kate Sheedy. The wheels of justice continued to turn as Bellfield was later charged with the murder of Marsha McDonnell on May 25, 2006.

Additional charges of abduction and attempted murder against Bellfield included the case of **Anna-Maria Rennie** in 2001 and **Irma Dragoshi** in 2003.

On February 25, 2008, Bellfield was found guilty of McDonnell and Delagrange's murders, as well as Sheedy's attempted murder. On March 30, 2010, Bellfield faced charges for Dowler's kidnapping and murder, along with the attempted kidnapping of **Rachel Cowles** the day before Dowler's disappearance. Despite Bellfield's denial of involvement, a jury convicted him of Milly Dowler's murder on June 23, 2011. He also received another life imprisonment sentence with a whole life order for Milly Dowler's abduction and murder.

Bellfield also emerged as a suspect in a series of unsolved murders and assaults on women dating back to 1980. Police believed that Bellfield could have been involved in approximately twenty other unsolved assaults on women in London spanning from 1990 to around 2004.

In early 2015, authorities received information that Bellfield, while incarcerated at HM Prison

Wakefield, had confessed to several other unsolved rape and murder cases. This revelation prompted the Metropolitan Police to coordinate investigations involving ten police forces.

In January 2016, Surrey Police announced Bellfield's admission to abducting, raping, and murdering Milly Dowler during an interview. Bellfield later disputed this, but the police maintained their statement.

However, on November 9, 2016, the police issued a statement declaring that all leads had been thoroughly pursued, resulting in the decision to close the investigation. They cited a lack of evidence linking Bellfield to additional cases beyond those for which he had already been convicted.

It was believed that Bellfield may have fabricated claims about other murders, potentially with the intent to inflict further anguish upon the families of the victims.

On June 16, 1980, **Patricia "Patsy" Joyce Morris**, a fourteen-year-old schoolgirl from Feltham, London, was strangled to death. She purportedly vanished during her lunch break to retrieve her forgotten raincoat from home. Two days later, her lifeless body was discovered by a police dog handler on Hounslow Heath, fully clothed and strangled with a ligature. Despite extensive investigations, no sexual assault was evident.

After his conviction in February 2008, the police announced their inquiry into a potential confession by Bellfield regarding Morris' murder. Allegedly fixated on the case since its occurrence, Bellfield divulged details to a fellow inmate while in custody. Further revelations revealed Bellfield's connection to Morris as her childhood boyfriend, having attended the same school. This revelation stunned Morris' family, who were unaware of the association. Bellfield, only twelve years old at the time of Morris' murder, was often absent from school and had a propensity for loitering on Hounslow Heath during school hours.

Former partners of Bellfield testified to his animosity toward blonde women, coincidentally aligning with Morris' appearance. Speculation arose that Morris' tragic demise may have sparked Bellfield's violent fixation on blondes.

George Morris, Patricia's father, recalled a chilling death threat received over the phone. He suspected Bellfield's involvement, given his proximity to the community and age at the time of the crime.

Bellfield's implication in Morris' murder underscored a potential dark genesis to his violent tendencies, signaling a disturbing trajectory that continued throughout his criminal career.

Authorities also disclosed their scrutiny of the murder of **Judith Gold**, a fifty-one-year-old woman from Hampstead, in October 1990. A middle-class housewife, Gold tragically perished just yards from her home, succumbing to multiple blows to the face from an unidentified weapon.

Police believed that Bellfield could have been involved in Gold's murder. This belief stemmed from the fact that their meticulous research into blunt-force trauma attacks revealed a rare occurrence of such crimes during that period. It also meant that only one case in the Greater London area was unattributed to Bellfield.

The circumstances surrounding Gold's murder remained perplexing. After leaving her residence above the Midland Bank in Hampstead High Street around 5:30 a.m. on the fateful day, Gold was dressed as if for a business meeting. She was discovered battered nearby by a paperboy in Old Brewery Mews amidst the darkness. Curiously, no witnesses reported any suspicious activity, and her sudden departure at that time of the night baffled her housemates.

Gold, known professionally as Judith Silver, juggled roles as an insurance and mortgage agent and a freelance financier. While her murder exhibited no signs of sexual assault, the motive appeared unrelated to a robbery. Her belongings were left untouched, except for a distinctive chain gifted to her by her younger boyfriend, which was missing.

Then, speculation arose regarding Gold's involvement in fraudulent loan schemes, suggesting a possible motive linked to an 'international financial swindle.' Investigators surmised that she may have arranged a clandestine meeting with her assailant, given her uncharacteristic early departure and involvement in shadowy financial dealings.

Gold's actions leading up to her death hinted that something strange was going on, including a mysterious reversal of her car in its parking space—something she never did. In February 2022, reports emerged alleging Bellfield's "confession" to Gold's murder, adding a new layer of complexity to the long-standing case.

Forty-five-year-old **Lin Russell** and her six-ycar-old daughter **Mcgan** were tragically murdered on July 9, 1996. *BBC Cymru Wales* reported an alleged confession by Bellfield to a fellow inmate, divulging details that could only be known to the perpetrator. But then Bellfield vehemently denied any involvement in the crime. A 2017 *BBC Two* program, *The Chillenden Murders*, supported re-investigating Bellfield's potential role in the killings, a stance also endorsed by the legal team of Michael Stone, the individual convicted of the crimes.

In December 2017, *The Sunday Times* reported that an alibi provided by Bellfield's ex-wife, Johanna Collings, placed him elsewhere at the time of the Russell murders. Collings attested that Bellfield spent the entire day with her in Twickenham and Windsor, a hundred miles away from the crime scene, during her 25th birthday celebration. Detectives found this alibi credible, particularly given Collings' prior cooperation in Bellfield's other convictions, such as in the Milly Dowler case.

Addressing the accusations in a 2017 *BBC* documentary, Collings reaffirmed Bellfield's presence with her throughout the day of the Russell murders, vehemently denying the possibility of his involvement. Despite subsequent claims by Stone's lawyer in February 2022, alleging Bellfield's confession in a four-page statement, skepticism arose regarding the authenticity of the details, with suggestions of fabrication using publicly available evidence. Detective Colin Sutton, familiar with Bellfield's behavior, suggested the possibility of manipulative tactics.

The Metropolitan Police previously investigated Bellfield's purported involvement in the Russell murders, ultimately finding no substantial evidence to support the allegations. However, in 2023, Bellfield's lawyer claimed he admitted to the crimes during a conversation with a prison psychologist, leading to the submission of a signed confession to the Criminal Cases Review Commission (CCRC). Though initially declining to refer the case to the Court of Appeal in July 2023, the CCRC reversed its decision three months later, initiating a review of Stone's conviction based on this new development.

In October 2022, authorities were alerted to Bellfield's confession regarding the abduction, rape, and murder of nineteen-year-old **Elizabeth Chau**, who vanished in 1999. Additionally, he confessed to attempting to murder five other women. Chau disappeared from West London on April 16, 1999, after leaving her West Ealing home to attend Thames Valley University. She was last seen by a friend at Ealing Broadway around 5:50 p.m. that day. Bellfield's confession remained undisclosed until April 2023.

After the revelation, Bellfield was formally interviewed regarding Chau's murder the following month, where he admitted to the abduction and killing, even pinpointing the location of her body on a map. However, the family of Chau accused the Metropolitan Police of neglecting the case due to racial bias. Authorities, nonetheless, assured they were treating Bellfield's claims with utmost gravity.

Coincidentally, twenty-seven-year-old **Lola Shenkoya** vanished from the exact location as Chau on Ealing Broadway on January 3, 2000. She was last spotted disembarking a bus near Ealing Broadway Underground Station. She has not been seen since. Shenkoya's case is presumed to be linked to Chau's disappearance. Despite the connection, Bellfield has not been publicly identified as a suspect in Shenkoya's presumed murder.

In January 2004, twenty-three-year-old **Sarah Spurrell** endured a harrowing ordeal when she was struck three times with a hammer in a dimly lit street in the East Sussex town of Hastings.

Thankfully, Spurrell survived the vicious attack thanks to the timely intervention of a bystander. However, her subsequent interaction with law enforcement left her disheartened, as she alleged being informed by police that they lacked the necessary resources to pursue an investigation into the assault. Spurrell expressed feelings of being dismissed by authorities, characterizing their response to her case as an "utter joke."

In March 2023, Bellfield, who had been identified as a suspect in the case since 2008, reportedly confessed to the attack on Spurrell, along with several other attempted murders and assaults. Spurrell was only informed of Bellfield's confession after being told by journalists working for *ITV News*. This revelation drew criticism toward the police for their handling of the matter.

Despite his incarceration, Bellfield's personal life continued to be tumultuous. Over his lifetime, he fathered eleven children with five different women, most recently with his girlfriend Emma Mills. In May 2022, the Ministry of Justice said that Bellfield was engaged and had applied for his marriage license in prison. This revelation sparked controversy, as he proposed to a woman who had corresponded with him for two years prior, eventually becoming a regular visitor. Any potential marriage would require the governor's permission at HM Prison Frankland, where Bellfield is still detained.

SIXTEEN

Colin Norris

ANGEL OF DEATH

Colin Norris was a Scottish serial killer and nurse who openly admitted his aversion to elderly patients and had a history of robbing hospital drugs. He was the sole staff member present when five elderly patients inexplicably lapsed into sudden hypoglycemic comas (i.e., low blood sugar). None of them had diabetes, and in fact, they were only admitted to the hospital for minor injuries like broken hips. Yet, they all experienced severe and sudden drops in blood sugar levels while in hospital.

Suspicion was raised when Norris eerily forecasted the demise of Ethel Hall, accurately predicting the time of her fatal episode. Tests later revealed she had been injected with an exceptionally high dose of artificial insulin. Later, it was discovered that a large amount of insulin was missing from the hospital fridge, and Norris was the nurse who had last accessed it only a half hour before Ethel died.

Later investigations revealed a pattern of suspicious hypoglycemic incidents following Norris' transfer to a second hospital. Records showed Norris as the common factor in all occurrences of deaths. After this, detectives decided to look into the deaths of seventy-two people while Norris was working. A special medical panel brought this number down to eighteen deaths for the police to investigate. In the end, detectives were able to pursue charges for six patients – four murders and two attempted murders. But they suspected Norris' involvement in up to six additional deaths where he was the only attendant. A lack of conclusive post-mortem evidence hindered any arrest, let alone convictions.

Norris is speculated to have drawn inspiration from Jessie McTavish, a Scottish nurse convicted of using insulin to murder a patient in 1974. McTavish's conviction was overturned in 1975. The incident occurred at Ruchill Hospital in Glasgow, less than a mile from Norris' childhood home. Norris became acquainted with McTavish's case shortly before completing his nursing qualifications.

Colin Campbell Norris was born on February 12, 1976, possibly in the Milton area of Glasgow, Scotland. After completing college, he was initially employed as a travel agent, but he opted to pursue a career in nursing. Friends characterized him as someone who relished being the center of attention, indulging in amateur dramatics. Despite his average academic performance, Norris gained notoriety for his quick temper and confrontational demeanor towards tutors and later employers. Constant arguments marked his contentious relationship with university lecturers at the University of Dundee.

Norris cited a personality clash with his tutor. Interestingly, this same tutor introduced Norris to the case of Jessie McTavish, a nurse implicated in a patient's death at Ruchill Hospital in Glasgow, a stone's throw away from Norris's childhood home. She was convicted of murdering a patient with insulin. McTavish's conviction was eventually overturned on appeal. It was believed that Norris' involvement in reviewing McTavish's case under his tutor's guidance ultimately led to his drawing inspiration from the case, particularly learning about the lethal potential of insulin as a murder weapon and its undetectability due to its rapid absorption into the bloodstream.

Following his graduation, Norris commenced work in Leeds in June 2001. As expected, he quickly clashed with authority figures, struggling with receiving instructions and unhappy to be working in minor injury wards and elderly care units. Expressing a preference for the emergency department due to its perceived excitement, Norris had conflicts with hospital management. Later, revelations surfaced regarding Norris' undercover work as a nurse in other hospitals on the same days when he called in sick or said he was off doing training.

Testimonies from Norris' former partner shed light on his increasingly volatile behavior. There were allegations of physical abuse, including hitting and hurling objects, which precipitated their breakup. Moreover, his fascination with a storyline from the television series *Holby City*, featuring a nurse serial killer, coupled with reports of experimenting on his pet cat with lethal insulin doses, further highlighted Norris' disturbing descent into violence. Despite his partner's report to the police, Norris evaded accountability. And he attributed the cat's demise to accidental trauma.

Subsequent investigations unveiled a pattern of mistreatment towards elderly patients during Norris' early nursing tenure at the same Leeds hospitals where he later perpetrated his crimes. In one distressing incident, an older man requested assistance emptying his catheter bag, only to encounter Norris' blunt refusal, insisting he manage it himself and just left for the day. Tragically, the man collapsed while attempting to reach the bathroom unaided.

Additional testimonies from patients revealed Norris' dismissive and indifferent demeanor towards elderly individuals, indicative of a deep-seated aversion. Two former patients recounted instances of verbal abuse from Norris after calling for emergency assistance for a fellow patient, with Norris hurling malicious remarks such as "I hope you suffer" and "rot in hell" at them.

A year after Norris obtained his nursing qualifications, he was employed at Leeds General Infirmary and St James' University Hospital in Leeds. Suspicion first arose when Norris predicted the death of a patient, Ethel Hall, confiding to a colleague mere hours beforehand, "I foresee 5:15 a.m. as the time Ethel Hall will take a turn for the worse." It unsettled the staff, given the fact that Ethel Hall was only admitted because of a fractured hip. She didn't show any signs of other illnesses. The alarming comments from Norris persisted, saying things like her being a "jinx" on the hospital and lamenting the paperwork that would accompany her eventual demise. When Hall indeed fell very ill around 5:00 a.m., and her condition proved fatal weeks later, Norris reminded a nurse of his earlier prediction, even further unsettling staff members.

Norris' carefree attitude about her sickness and his delayed response during Hall's collapse irked attending medical professionals. It even made them suspicious, so much so that a blood sample was drawn from Hall and sent to the lab for examination. The test unveiled an extraordinarily high level of insulin—1000 units —in her system, a stark anomaly given her lack of medical need for such dosage. This discovery, indicative of foul play, prompted hospital authorities to involve law enforcement. Subsequent investigations revealed insulin theft from storage, with Norris confessing to being the last individual to access the fridge before Hall's insulin injection. Additionally, Norris admitted being the last to interact with Hall before her sudden deterioration, coinciding with the onset of her coma at approximately 5:00 a.m.

These facts about Norris prompted a broader investigation into the deaths of 72 individuals under his care during his shifts. A panel of medical experts convened to review those cases and concluded that 18 of those deaths should be investigated by the police as suspicious deaths.

Corroborating police suspicions, they confirmed that three other women had indeed fallen victim to lethal insulin injections, and two more victims could have − one died of insulin poisoning, and one survived the overdose. Notably, none of these women, including Hall, had diabetes and no need for an insulin injection. They were admitted to non-emergency orthopedic wards for minor injuries like fractured hips.

The disturbing pattern of events commenced at Leeds General Infirmary in May 2002, coinciding with the conclusion of Norris's probationary monitoring as a newly qualified nurse. On multiple occasions, Norris administered unwarranted morphine doses followed by insulin injections, usually at the end of his shifts.

In that year, Norris was transferred to St James's University Hospital, and it wasn't long before they saw a recurrence of similar incidents, implicating Norris as the sole common denominator in these mysterious hypoglycaemic attacks. Witnesses recounted Norris' indifferent demeanor during these critical moments, casting further suspicion on him.

Norris seemingly felt encouraged to continue his actions undetected, assuming blood tests wouldn't be conducted to reveal insulin overdoses. His choice of victims, predominantly labeled by him as "difficult" patients, suggests a disturbing correlation with his disdain for elderly individuals. Each incident seemed to occur during Norris' night shifts, coinciding with the absence of supervisory medical staff. He made chilling remarks about fatalities occurring during his night shifts, and his colleagues' observations point to a calculated modus operandi. The victims shared common vulnerabilities, including frailty and admission for minor injuries like broken hips, further highlighting Norris' targeted approach.

It was determined that Norris was the sole nurse attending to all five patients within two hours of their sudden illnesses, and he was among the few on duty during Hall's decline. Police scrutinized medical staff schedules, phone logs, and records to ascertain ward access, insulin handling, and staffing during critical moments. Only Norris was always present during the incidents, working across both affected wards. Although Norris admitted predicting Hall's death to a colleague during questioning, he dismissed it as dark humor. When the body of one of his victims, Bridget Bourke, was exhumed, it revealed significant insulin levels. The other deceased patients had been cremated, hindering further testing.

Norris was suspended with pay while the police investigated. After he was arrested and released, he hastily left Leeds and traveled abroad eight times, including an extended stay in Tenerife. His partner recounted instances of violent behavior but excused it as fear of imprisonment. His mother defended his European travels to cope with the investigation's pressure.

Norris suggested an intruder's involvement when questioned about missing insulin vials despite no evidence of a break-in or prior sightings of the vials. During questioning, Norris became aggressive and arrogant and even had to be restrained once. He neither explicitly denied nor admitted to the murders but challenged the police's evidence. Criminologist Dr. Jane Monkton-Smith noted Norris' behavior, suggesting a desire to display superiority. In 2004, Norris asserted his innocence to reporters.

Chief Superintendent Chris Gregg interpreted Norris' prediction of Hall's illness as premeditation rather than spontaneity, suggesting arrogance and overconfidence. A criminal psychologist asserted that Norris wasn't seeking capture by making Hall's death prediction, but instead, he desired to flaunt knowledge. Norris' lack of empathy towards the victims and their families surely implicated him.

Norris faced trial in 2007 at Newcastle Crown Court. Despite his father's harsh condemnation of him as "scum," Norris adamantly denied ever predicting Hall's death and contradicted earlier admissions made during police interviews. However, he confessed to administering overdoses of morphine to Vera Wilby and Doris Ludlam. Police noted Norris' deliberate omission of Ludlam, Bourke, and Crooke during initial questioning, suggesting an attempt to avoid suspicion before investigators discovered they were victims.

During the trial, evidence emerged of documents found at Norris' residence outlining less painful methods of morphine injection. Norris maintained that none of the patients had been injected despite blood test results. He continued to insist on the involvement of an intruder despite secure access to the insulin fridge from which the drug was taken.

On March 3, 2008, Norris was found guilty by an 11-1 majority vote for the murders of four women and the attempted murder of one. The four individuals he killed were Doris Ludlam on June 27, 2002; 88-year-old Bridget Bourke on July 22, 2002; 79-year-old Irene Crooke on October 20, 2002; and Ethel Hall on December 11, 2002. He attempted to murder 90-year-old Vera Wilby on May 17, 2002, as well. Norris received a life sentence the following day. He was ordered to serve a minimum of thirty years behind bars.

Throughout the trial, Norris displayed aggression, even assaulting members of the press upon exiting the court. Restrictions on televised coverage were necessary to prevent jury influence. The judge admonished Norris during sentencing:

"You are, without a doubt, a profoundly wicked and dangerous individual. Your demeanor exudes arrogance and manipulation, particularly evident in your disdain for elderly patients. The poignant testimony of Bridget Tarpey, expressing 'he did not like us old women,' encapsulates this sentiment. It appears you harbored resentment towards them due to their increased need for care and attention, revealing a fundamental laziness, as evidenced by your frequent absences from student placements and work."

In stark contrast, Norris' mother, June Morrison, expressed immense pride in her son, claiming she was "so proud of him."

Dubbed the "Angel of Death" by the British

press, these tragic murders occurred during Norris' first year as a nurse. Ethal Hall was a mother and grandmother. Doris Ludlam was a mother, grandmother, and great-grandmother who had devoted her life to teaching and fostering children. Vera Wilby was a vulnerable widow, and Irene Crooke passed away on her 79th birthday and denied the joy of opening her birthday cards and gifts.

Ethal Hall's son, Stuart, expressed relief at Norris' conviction, emphasizing the necessity of his incarceration for the safety of society. He stressed Norris' dangerous ability to discreetly execute lethal acts, underscoring the imperative of keeping him behind bars indefinitely.

Following the verdict, Leeds Teaching Hospitals NHS Trust apologized to the victim's families for the distress caused by Norris' "disturbing" crimes and labeled him an "extremely dangerous criminal." In 2009, the Nursing and Midwifery Council quickly revoked Norris' medical license, affirming his expulsion from the profession.

As of 2019, Norris remains incarcerated in HM Prison Frankland.

After the trial, Detective Chris Gregg disclosed that he and fellow detectives suspected Norris of involvement in as many as six additional deaths at the hospitals. Norris was the sole nurse present during three other suspicious deaths, though insufficient evidence hindered police efforts to secure convictions for those incidents. Furthermore, Norris had faced arrest in connection with another patient's death, but the Crown Prosecution Service opted against pressing charges due to "complicating factors." In two other suspicious death cases, the absence of post-mortem examinations impeded the accumulation of evidence necessary to charge Norris for those fatalities.

As for the motive, some claim that Jessie McTavish, a nurse initially convicted and later controversially acquitted of the 1974 murder of an 80-year-old patient using insulin, was the probable inspiration for Norris. She was employed at Ruchill Hospital in Glasgow, less than a mile from Norris' childhood home. McTavish's release on appeal followed a successful argument from her defense team, who claimed that the judge mistakenly misled the jury in his final summation, despite the appeal court judges acknowledging that this was something "a few words could have cured" and that there was sufficient evidence to support the prosecution.

A significant event preceding Norris' first attack was a lecture given to him and fellow students by his university tutor on McTavish's case on January 11, 2001. Norris replicated the method allegedly used by McTavish in his initial attempt. Tasked with "reviewing" McTavish's conduct, Norris likely learned that insulin was an effective murder weapon due to its rapid elimination from the bloodstream. Similar to Norris, McTavish had eerily "predicted" the exact time of a patient's demise. Astonishingly, despite her legal ordeal, McTavish was able to resume her nursing career after her release.

Forensic psychiatrist Sir Richard Badcock, renowned for his assessment of the serial killer doctor Harold Shipman, classified Norris as a psychopath. Badcock believed Norris targeted elderly patients simply because they obstructed his objectives. Norris' motive mirrored that of Shipman's. Detective Chris Gregg speculated that Norris poisoned women out of sheer irritation with elderly patients. Dr. David Holmes, a Psychologist at Manchester Metropolitan University, surmised that Norris sought power through his actions, using his medical role to assert dominance over life and death. High-profile criminologist David Wilson contextualized Norris' case within a trend of emerging vulnerabilities among certain groups to serial attacks.

In 2009, Norris initiated an appeal against his conviction. Initially, he intended to challenge the trial judge's perceived bias but later abandoned this course of action, dismissing his legal team. Instead, he pursued an appeal based on alleged jury misdirection by the judge during his final summary.

However, this appeal was unsuccessful. In presiding over the case, Judge Lord Justice Aikens upheld Norris' convictions, deeming them "secure" and remarking on the strength of the evidence against him. The appeal court dismissed both grounds of appeal, asserting that the judge's instructions to the jury were beyond reproach, labeling his original summary as a masterful exposition. The judges also rejected the notion of the deaths being coincidental. Norris' defense asserted that naturally elevated insulin levels might have caused the deaths due to spontaneous hypoglycemia, but this argument was also rejected.

The Criminal Case Review Commission

(CCRC) received information questioning the accuracy of the test results, indicating Ethel Hall's bloodstream was saturated with insulin, casting doubt on the possibility of her being murdered by an insulin overdose. However, in 2021, the commission refuted this claim, affirming that Hall was indeed murdered by insulin injection. Despite this, the CCRC acknowledged that Norris' conviction for Hall's murder was dependent on the support from the other four convictions and the prosecution's assertion that Norris acted alone. With new expert evidence, the commission expressed uncertainty regarding the allegation that Norris was solely responsible for Hall's murder.

In 2010, an independent inquiry delved into Norris' string of murders. Among its recommendations was the implementation of 'student practice passports,' designed to assess the character and integrity of aspiring medical professionals during their university training. It was believed that such passports could have potentially identified Norris' problematic behavior earlier, given his history of aggression during placements, frequent absenteeism, and clashes with tutors. Advocates argued that these passports would enable universities to evaluate a student's suitability for entry into the medical profession upon completion of their course.

The inquiry uncovered that the University of Dundee had failed to recognize Norris' issues in its references to prospective employers. It concluded that organizational, systemic, and cultural factors created an environment conducive for Norris to commit the 2002 murders. Following Norris' conviction in 2008, nurse managers had already been urged to exercise greater caution in staff recruitment, prompting NHS Employers to introduce new guidelines on pre-employment screenings.

On October 4, 2011, the *BBC* reported that retired Professor Vincent Marks, a leading authority on insulin poisoning, expressed concerns about Norris' conviction. Marks, commissioned by Norris' family to investigate, contended that experts had misled the jury into viewing a series of hypoglycemic episodes among non-diabetic individuals as suspicious. After conducting his research, Marks concluded that Norris' conviction was potentially unsafe, highlighting his findings that up to 1 in 10 hypoglycemic episodes in elderly individuals occurred naturally. Marks pointed out that the four patients singled out by experts following Mrs. Hall's death were all highly susceptible to spontaneous hypoglycemia due to various risk factors such as malnutrition, infection, and multi-organ failure.

Norris' mother has tirelessly advocated for her son's innocence, claiming that she was the mother of Scotland's worst serial killer or the mother of a victim of a grave miscarriage of justice. However, most family members of the victims remain convinced of Norris' guilt.

In 2013, the CCRC decided to take another look at Norris' case in light of new medical and scientific evidence contradicting what was presented at trial. However, there was public outrage when a benefit concert for Norris was held in Dundee, with critics condemning the event as disrespectful to the victims' families.

Amidst ongoing debate and controversy, the foreman of Norris' jury, upon reviewing evidence presented in the *BBC* program, expressed a belief in Norris' innocence. In January 2015, he joined another juror in that assessment, though most jurors still upheld Norris' conviction.

In February 2021, the CCRC announced its decision to refer the case to the Court of Appeal, citing severe doubts about the safety of Norris' conviction. Regarding Ethel Hall's case, the CCRC affirmed her murder by insulin injection.

However, experts advising the commission could not entirely rule out the possibility of natural hypoglycemia in the other four cases, despite Norris' defense team's assertion of natural deaths. The CCRC emphasized the invaluable input of the defense team's experts in reaching their decision.

SEVENTEEN

Anthony Hardy

THE CAMDEN RIPPER

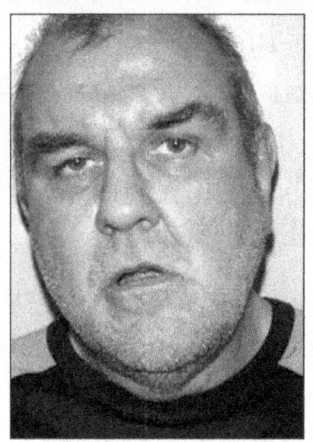

A nthony John Hardy was born in Burton upon Trent, Staffordshire, on May 31, 1951. Hardy enjoyed a seemingly unremarkable childhood and excelled academically throughout school and college. He obtained an engineering degree from Imperial College London and later assumed a managerial position at a prominent company.

Hardy eventually married and had three sons and one daughter, though his personal life was marred by turmoil. In 1982, he faced arrest in Tasmania for an attempted drowning of his wife, but the charges were ultimately dismissed.

Following their divorce in 1986, Hardy's mental health deteriorated, leading to stays in mental hospitals where he was diagnosed with bipolar disorder. He also underwent treatment for depression, drug-induced psychosis, and alcohol abuse in various psychiatric facilities across London. His life took a downward spiral, marked by stints in hostels and brushes with the law. These events resulted in convictions for theft and disorderly conduct, as well as an accusation of rape by a prostitute in 1998. He was not formally charged with the rape due to insufficient evidence. After this, he struggled with alcoholism and diabetes.

In January 2002, police responded to a complaint from a neighbor living in the same block of flats as Hardy. She asserted her front door was vandalized and implicated Hardy. When the police went to question Hardy at his flat, they discovered a locked room. Despite Hardy's denial of having a key, they found one. Inside the room, they found the lifeless body of Sally White, 38, a prostitute residing in London, naked on a bed with evidence of head injuries.

Forensic pathologist Freddy Patel initially attributed White's death to a heart attack, a conclusion later questioned when Patel's professional conduct came to light. His handling of this murder case and others, including the controversial 2009 death of Ian Tomlinson, led to his temporary suspension from the government's register of pathologists pending an inquiry. In 2012, Patel was permanently removed from the medical register by the General Medical Council, prohibiting him from practicing medicine in the United Kingdom.

Hardy eventually confessed to a charge of criminal damage but professed ignorance regarding how White came to be in his flat, citing his alcoholism as the reason. He was arrested and taken into custody but was subsequently transferred to a psychiatric hospital and remained there until November 2002.

On December 30, 2002, a homeless man going through the garbage cans outside businesses and homes found what looked like disposed food scraps sealed in plastic bags. But when he opened them, he saw female body parts inside. Police were able to identify the remains belonging to thirty-four-year-old Bridgette MacClennan and twenty-nine-year-old Elizabeth Valad.

Hardy was arrested a week later for their murders at the University Hospital. He was seen by two undercover officers when he went into the pharmacy to pick up his prescription for insulin. Before they could arrest him, Hardy noticed the two men and ran outside. They found him hiding behind the hospital garbage bins at the back of the property.

Hardy wouldn't give up easily and began fighting the two officers. During the scuffle, he knocked one of the officers out, grabbed a knife from his pocket, and began stabbing the other officer. Hardy sliced the officer's hand open before stabbing him in his left eye so hard that it came out of the socket. But even with the severe injuries, the officer was able to secure Hardy until more police arrived at the scene.

During his interview, Hardy only answered the officers' questions with one sentence: "No comment." He was formally charged with the murders of MacClennan and Valad. They also charged him with the murder of Sally White, which they initially believed was a death by natural causes.

After the trial began in November 2003, Hardy began to talk and plead guilty to all three of the murder charges. He was convicted and given a sentence of life in prison. The court also ordered another psychiatric evaluation, which diagnosed him as having a personality disorder. As a result of this, the court decided that Hardy needed to stay in prison for the rest of his life.

After his conviction, authorities speculated on Hardy's potential involvement in unsolved cases, including those of two prostitutes found dismembered and discarded in the River Thames. Additionally, there were similarities between Hardy's convicted crimes and five or six other murders. However, there was no evidence directly linking him to these cases, which hindered further investigation.

The first murder police believed might be associated with Hardy was Paula Fields, a prostitute in London whose body was found in the Thames in 2001. But, in 2011, the case was solved, and John Sweeney was proven to be her killer.

The murder of Zoe Parker was also thought to have been committed by Hardy because her dismembered torso was discovered in the river. The lower half of Parker's body was never recovered, and investigators believed it had been dismembered with a sharp instrument, possibly a Samurai sword. The press noted potential connections between Hardy and the Parker case shortly after his arrest in January 2003.

Twenty-four-year-old Zoe Parker's remains were found on December 17, 2000, eleven days after her disappearance, next to Chelsea Harbour on the Thames. Zoe, also known as Cathy Dennis, was a sex worker who frequented areas in west London, including Isleworth, Feltham, Hounslow, and occasionally the West End. She was described as friendly, often engaging in conversations with strangers. On the night of her disappearance, she was seen in Hounslow by two white men with dark hair. One wore a white casual jacket, dark trousers, and white trainers, while the other was stocky and dressed in dark clothing. Investigators appealed for a woman named Carmen or Carmel to come forward, believing she had information about the murder and was a friend of Parker's from the Hounslow or Isleworth area.

On November 25, 2020, Hardy passed away from pneumonia at HM Prison Frankland in County Durham at the age of 69.

EIGHTEEN

Mark Martin

THE SNEINTON STRANGLER

Mark Martin is a British serial killer known in the media as the "Sneinton Strangler." He has been sentenced to a whole-life order, meaning he will never be released from prison. His two accomplices, John Ashley and Dean Carr, assisted him in two murders and received minimum sentences of twenty-five years and fourteen years, respectively.

Mark Martin was born in Ilkeston, Derbyshire, England on October 18, 1979. He was an only child and endured extensive bullying at school due to a prominent birthmark under his left eye. His father was imprisoned during Martin's childhood and allegedly shared a prison with the infamous organized crime figures, the Kray Twins.

By age sixteen, the younger Martin had turned to petty crime. He married in his early twenties, but the marriage ended after he violently attacked his wife in 2002, and they separated in 2004. After the separation, Martin became homeless and lived on the streets of Nottingham.

He, along with fellow criminals John Ashley and Dean Carr, was feared among Nottingham's homeless community, frequently stealing from their peers. Martin, often called "Reds," and Ashley, known as "Cockney John," were infamous. Martin was described as the "leader of the pack." He was characterized as a violent, volatile, and aggressive bully with a short temper.

Reportedly, Martin sought fame and notoriety,

openly boasting that his ambition was to become "Nottingham's first serial killer." On the night of January 24, 2005, Martin, along with Ashley, Carr, and another homeless woman, twenty-five-year-old Ellen Frith, were in a run-down flat on Marple Road in Nottingham. This flat was a well-known gathering spot for the homeless to assemble and take drugs. At some point in the evening, Frith began eating an apple when Martin suddenly grabbed her by the throat and strangled her to death. He then injected her leg with a syringe before setting the property on fire and escaping with his friends. Firefighters extinguished the blaze and discovered Frith's body inside.

A man who had been in the flat the previous night informed the police that Martin, Ashley, and Carr were present with Frith on the night of her death. Investigators confirmed that the three men were at the flat when the fire started. The police apprehended Ashley, who admitted witnessing Martin strangle Frith. Two days later, Martin called the police, boasting, "I think you want me for murder," but he wasn't apprehended right away. Dean Carr was arrested later but claimed that both Martin and Ashley had killed Frith.

When Martin was finally arrested and questioned, he responded to all police inquiries with "No comment." Both he and Ashley were charged with Frith's murder.

During subsequent interviews, Martin hinted at his involvement in other murders. Upon investigation, witnesses provided names of two other homeless women who had recently disappeared from the city and had not been seen since December 2004: eighteen-year-old Katie Baxter and twenty-six-year-old Zoe Pennick.

Katie Baxter had been in a violent relationship with Ashley. Investigators uncovered that Martin had lured Baxter to his tent with the promise of 2,000 cigarettes before strangling her. Zoe Pennick was last seen on December 31, 2004.

Members of the homeless community came forward, reporting that Martin had boasted about killing both Pennick and Baxter and in February 2005, police discovered both bodies under rubble near Martin's tent. Forensic analysis determined that both women had died between December 30, 2004, and January 6, 2005.

Charges for the murders of Pennick and Baxter were added to Mark Martin and John Ashley, while the charges against Ashley for Frith's murder were dropped. Dean Carr was charged with Frith's murder but not with the other killings.

In January 2006, all three men stood trial at

Nottingham Crown Court. Several homeless witnesses testified about the defendants' confessions, leading to their convictions despite their not-guilty pleas.

Carr received a life sentence with a minimum term of fourteen years for his involvement in Frith's murder. Ashley was given a minimum twenty-five-year sentence for his role in two of the murders. On February 23, 2008, Martin, identified as the ringleader, was sentenced to life imprisonment with a whole-life order after being convicted of three murders. The judge wanted to ensure Martin would never be released. Martin was one of approximately fifty prisoners to have been issued whole-life tariffs.

NINETEEN

Steve Wright

THE SUFFOLK STRANGLER

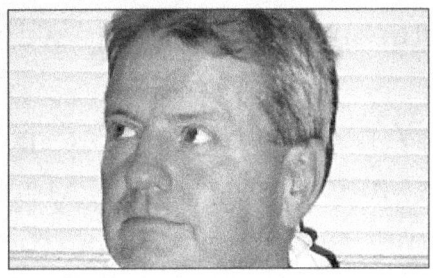

S teven Gerald James Wright is an English serial killer, also known as "The Suffolk Strangler." He is serving life imprisonment for the murders of five female sex workers in Ipswich, Suffolk. The murders occurred during the final months of 2006. Wright was found guilty in February 2008 and received a whole-life order, ensuring he would never be released from prison.

Early Life

Steve Wright was born on April 24, 1958, in the Norfolk village of Erpingham. He was the second of four children to military policeman Conrad Wright and a veterinary nurse, Patricia. The family had two boys and two girls. They lived in Malta and Singapore during his father's military service. Wright's mother left the family in 1964 when he was six. His parents divorced in 1978, and they later found new spouses. Wright and his siblings lived with their father, who had two more children, a son and a daughter, with his second wife, Valerie.

In 1974, Wright left school at sixteen without qualifications and joined the Merchant Navy, becoming a chef on ferries sailing from Felixstowe, Suffolk. In 1978, at age twenty, he married Angela O'Donovan in Milford Haven, Pembrokeshire, Wales. The couple had a son, Michael, before separating and divorcing in 1987. Wright held various jobs, including steward on the ocean liner Queen Elizabeth II, lorry driver, barman, and, then shortly before his arrest, forklift truck driver.

Wright's second marriage was to Diane Cassell at the Braintree, Essex, register office in August 1987, but this marriage, too, ended in divorce in

July 1988. During this time, he also managed a pub in South London but lost his job due to his gambling and heavy drinking.

By the late 1990s, Wright had accumulated large gambling debts and was declared bankrupt. He attempted suicide twice: first by carbon monoxide poisoning in his car in 1994 and then by an overdose of pills in 2000.

In 2001, Wright was convicted of theft for stealing £80 to pay off debts. It was his only criminal conviction before the murders, even though former prostitute Lindi St Clair claimed that Wright attacked her in the 1980s.

Later, Wright openly admitted to using prostitutes, a habit he developed during his time in the Merchant Navy and continued throughout his life. He admitted to visiting specific massage and sauna establishments that operated as brothels. During his trial, Wright confessed to frequenting prostitutes, including three of the murder victims.

Also in 2001, Wright met Pamela Wright (no relation) in Felixstowe, and they moved to Ipswich together in 2004. When Pamela started working night shifts and their sex life waned, Wright resumed paying for sex with at least a dozen women in the final three months of 2006.

Ipswich Serial Murders

Up to thirty young women plied their trade as sex workers to curb crawlers on a few isolated backstreets in Ipswich. During the three months between October and December 2006, the bodies of five murdered women were discovered near Ipswich in Suffolk, England. Forensic evidence led to Wright's arrest on December 19th after police confirmed the specks of blood found on the back seats of Wright's Ford Mondeo partially matched the DNA profile of murder victim Paula Clennell. Wright was found guilty of all five murders on February 21, 2008. The following day, at Ipswich Crown Court, Justice Gross sentenced Wright to life imprisonment and recommended that Wright never be released. On March 19, 2008, Wright appealed his convictions but later announced that he had decided to drop the appeal.

Victims

Nineteen-year-old **Tania Nicol** had been working the streets for over a year to fund her addiction to heroin and cocaine, and on the night of October 30th, she left home around 11:00 p.m. to start work. But that night, Tania failed to return home. Twenty-four hours later, her mother, unaware of her daughter's prostitution, reported her missing.

The Ipswich news media reported her missing person status. "This is 19-year-old Tania Nicol. She's been missing for over a week. Police are extremely concerned for her welfare because of her lifestyle."

It's not uncommon for people to go missing; more than 200,000 cases are reported every year. But in this instance, the police stated that alarm bells began ringing almost immediately.

"We knew Tania was a prostitute. We knew she was a working girl and was already considered high-risk. She's working in a high-risk industry; she's vulnerable. On her regular schedule, we would know that she was around; she would contact somebody. When she didn't, we knew we were dealing with quite a serious case."

Because of these fears, the police decided to

make a public appeal in the hope that someone, somewhere, knew where Tania was.

"Unfortunately, in the investigation so far, we haven't managed to locate her on any of the buses she may have caught into town, and we haven't located her on any available CCTV to date. A worried mother waits for news of her daughter. Anyone who can help should call Suffolk Police or Crimestoppers."

Tania Nicol's disappearance may have made news in Ipswich, but the story barely registered on the radar of any newspaper or TV station outside of Suffolk. But that would soon change because, before long, another woman would go missing under the same circumstances.

Gemma Adams was just twenty-five years old. She had been working the streets for two years, but after going out on the night of November 14th, she wasn't seen again. Like Tania Nicol,

Gemma regularly contacted friends to tell them about her whereabouts, but suddenly, those calls stopped. For the Suffolk police, this was an ominous sign. Soon, they stepped up their efforts to find both women.

"We distributed some 20,000 leaflets around the area. We set up road checks at periodic times after the disappearances, and we interviewed some 400 people in respect of Tania's disappearance and some 300 in respect of Gemma's disappearance."

But the leafleting campaign produced no leads, and police became increasingly pessimistic about finding either of the women alive. Along with their appeals for sightings, they began looking for bodies.

Two weeks later, on December 2nd, a passerby came across Gemma Adams's remains by the side of a dark, isolated brook. She was found naked in a brook but had not been sexually assaulted.

Adams was born in Kesgrave and lived in Ipswich. As a child, she was popular among her friends and affluent family. Nevertheless, as a teenager, she started down the road to addiction, eventually becoming addicted to heroin. She had been working as a prostitute to cover the cost of her drug addiction, which had already led to her being dismissed from her job with an insurance firm.

Police reported, "When Gemma was found, I think we went into shock. We all thought that we had two missing women, but we were confident that we would find them. That's when it started to hit home that we were dealing with a murder case."

With one sex worker dead and another missing, local reporters descended on the red-light district. There, they found girls frightened to work but unwilling to give up.

"Going out there, thinking, 'Is it my turn tonight? Am I not going to come home tonight?' You know what I mean? But what choice do I have but to go out there? So, you're in a dilemma. If you don't go

out there, you'll be ill. If you go out there,
you're going to be terrified."

After finding the first body, the police
extended their search for Tania, and six days later,
they found her. Like Gemma, she was discovered
in Belstead Brook and had been murdered. Suffolk
Constabulary, which dealt with an average of six
murders in an entire year, now had two in the
space of six days. Whoever was responsible
seemed to pick out girls randomly from Ipswich's
red-light district.

The sleepy county of Suffolk had become the
scene of one of Britain's most extensive
investigations. Two women had been found dead
after going missing on the streets of Ipswich, and
although their bodies were both discovered in the
same river, detectives were unable to establish a
definite link. But if there was any doubt that the
deaths were linked, it was soon to be removed.

Despite a high police presence on the streets,
Suffolk Constabulary was getting more reports of

women disappearing, and just days after the second body was found, a third was also discovered. This time, the victim was twenty-four-year-old **Anneli Alderton**, and like the others, she had been working as a prostitute. The police stated, "Once Anneli Alderton's body had been found, then clearly we were into a different realm, and it looked at that stage very much that we'd got a serial killer on our hands. We'd got very, very linked murder investigations in a very close area around Ipswich, and all the indications at that stage where it was the work of one man or a man or men working together in sort of a spree of killing."

Because Anneli's body was found on dry land, the police felt they had a better chance of finding valuable evidence. The head of crime scenes, David Stagg, was responsible for recovering it. As the forensic officers got to work, the investigation team came to terms with the new enormity of the case. A small force like Suffolk was ill-equipped to deal with a serial killer. Stagg claimed, "There probably wasn't an hour that went past where I wasn't thinking, "How many more? What else are we going to find?" because it was just escalating at such a rate. We lacked the staff, the number of police officers, and the police staff to assist us in putting all the different things we needed to do in place." Of the 43 police forces in England and Wales, 40 sent help. More than 100 members of the Forensic Science Service were also drafted in. Stagg and his team were under pressure to find clues pointing to the killer, but it wasn't proving easy.

Meanwhile, detectives began piecing together Anneli's last known movements. They discovered she had traveled by train from Harwich to work in Ipswich's red-light district on the night she disappeared. They found some CCTV footage of her traveling on the train and the platform at Manningtree before traveling to Ipswich. They confirmed that she visited her mother before leaving Essex and wanted to raise money to buy Christmas presents.

However, there was something more significant about these CCTV images. The date on the film showed they were captured on December 3rd, the day after the first body—that of Gemma Adams—was found. That meant the killer was not only on the loose; he was also operating right under the noses of the police. As a result, the police very quickly set up a presence in the red-light district. One slip-up, one foul move, and the killer would have been caught red-handed.

Popular opinion was the question of how this could happen, especially with all the CCTV cameras and officers patrolling the streets. It wasn't just the public asking those questions; the media were, too. They were descending on Suffolk in force, and as the number of victims grew, so did the number of cameras. Interest in the story suddenly mushroomed, and it became enormous overnight. One of the smallest forces in the country was now dealing with an unprecedented killing spree.

In the days that followed, more sex workers disappeared. Twenty-nine-year-old **Annette Nicholls** went missing on December 5th, and on December 10th, twenty-four-year-old **Paula Clennell** disappeared. Paula had given a TV interview on the streets of Ipswich less than a week before:

"Why have you decided to come out tonight?" a reporter asked.

"Because I need the money. I need the money, you know," replied Paula.

"You know, despite the dangers?"

"Well, that has made me a bit wary about getting into cars."

"But presumably, you will do that tonight?"

"Well, probably," she admitted.

On December 12th, when police were searching for clues in the wooded area where the third victim had been found, they found the bodies of Paula Clennell and Annette Nicholls.

According to Suffolk Police, Paula died from "compression of the throat." Her body was found naked, but not sexually assaulted. Paula was the mother of three children and was born in Northumberland. Her three children had all been taken into care due to her drug addiction. As a child, she had spent some time in a referral unit, and shortly after being placed there, she started taking drugs.

A friend of Paula's reported, "I saw Paula a few hours before she went out that night. I'm like, 'Well, make sure you look after yourself with all these people out there.' She's like, 'Don't worry; I'll just stay near on these streets, so I'll be safe; I'll be seen.' But then she didn't come back the next day."

Annette Nicholls was a mother of one from Ipswich. She, too, was found naked but not sexually assaulted. Her body was one of those posed in the cruciform position. Nicholls, the oldest victim, had been a drug addict since the early 2000s when she was completing a beautician's course at Suffolk College. Soon afterward, she started working as a prostitute to fund her addiction.

Other Possible Murders

Wright remains under investigation in connection with other unsolved murders and disappearances. Experts have pointed out that it's unlikely for any serial killer to begin killing at such a late stage in life, as serial killers typically start before their mid-thirties. Wright was forty-eight years old when the murders in 2006 were committed, suggesting he may have killed before. Psychologists who spoke to police after the murders stated it was "highly likely" he had previous victims.

Wright was among several high-profile murderers and sex offenders considered as possible suspects in the Suzy Lamplugh murder case. He had worked with Lamplugh on the Queen Elizabeth II in the early 1980s. Lamplugh disappeared somewhere in London in July 1986, and even though she was legally declared dead in 1994, her body has never been found. Even though Wright is a possible suspect, the Metropolitan Police have stated that Wright is not a strong line of inquiry in this case, and in 2002, police named John Cannan as the prime suspect in Lamplugh's disappearance.

A former police officer linked Wright to the murder of Jeanette Kempton in 1989. Kempton disappeared from Brixton, near where Wright lived at the time, and her body was found many miles away in a rural area of Suffolk.

In July 2021, Wright was arrested at HM Prison Long Lartin and charged with the 1999 murder of seventeen-year-old Victoria Hall, who was killed on her way home from a Suffolk nightclub. Five days after she was last seen alive in Felixstowe, Hall's body was found in a ditch. There wasn't enough evidence to bring it to trial, so the investigation was closed. But later, the Suffolk Police reopened their investigation after receiving new witness information. In December 2023, he was rearrested in connection with Victoria Hall's murder, and on May 22, 2024, he was charged with her murder as well as the attempted kidnapping of another woman.

Cleveland Police have not ruled out the possibility that Steve Wright murdered Vicky Glass, a factory worker from Middlesbrough who disappeared in September 2000. Her naked body was found in a brook on the North York Moors.

Wright has also been implicated in the cluster of unsolved sex worker murders in Norwich, where he previously lived and worked, and frequently returned to visit after moving to Ipswich. Criminologist David Wilson, who was involved with the investigations, agreed with other professionals and felt that the murders were far too practiced for someone murdering for the first time.

Wright was linked to the unsolved murders of:

- 16-year-old Natalie Pearman, Norwich, 1992
- 26-year-old Amanda Duncan, Ipswich, 1993
- 28 year old Kellie Pratt, Norwich, 2000

- 22-year-old Michelle Bettles, Norwich, 2002

Norwich sex worker Natalie Pearman was murdered in November 1992. She was last seen at night soliciting clients outside the Ferry Boat Inn Pub, the pub owned and run by Wright and located in the heart of the city's red light district. The police cross-referenced the DNA found on her body in 1992 to Wright's, but the results were "inconclusive."

Ipswich sex worker Amanda Duncan disappeared after talking to a man in a car on Portman Road in July 1993. Portman Road is where Wright was known to acquire his prostitutes and from where some of his victims were known to have disappeared in 2006.

Kellie Pratt was last seen on June 11, 2000, outside The Rose Pub in Queens Road, Norwich. Pratt received a phone call within ten minutes of being seen outside the pub. According to the person she was talking to, she was with "a punter," but the client she was with remains unknown, and no further clues were found. Neither her body nor her phone has ever been found. Unfortunately, neither has a link to Steve Wright. But her disappearance fell within a timeline of three other murders of women.

In June 2012, Criminologist Wilson suggested that Wright was likely the killer of Norwich sex worker Michelle Bettles. Police replied by stating they found no evidence connecting Wright to the crime. They had arrested another man back in April 2003 whose DNA matched samples from Bettles' body. This man admitted to picking her up for sex two days before she was last seen. But he claimed that on the night of her death, he was at home with a migraine, despite phone records showing him making numerous calls that evening. On March 28, 2022, police announced they had recovered further DNA profiles in Bettles' murder case, indicating Wright could be ruled out of the murder with forensic evidence.

TWENTY

Stephen Griffiths

THE CROSSBOW CANNIBAL

Stephen Shaun Griffiths was charged and convicted with what became known as "The Bradford Murders," referring to the murder and dismemberment of three women in the city of Bradford, Yorkshire, England, in 2009 and 2010. Griffiths was born on December 24, 1969, in Dewsbury, West Riding of Yorkshire.

Victims in the Bradford Murders were forty-three-year-old **Susan Rushworth**, who disappeared on June 22, 2009, followed by thirty-one-year-old **Shelley Armitage** on April 26, 2010, and thirty-six-year-old **Suzanne Blamires** on May 21st of the same year. All three women were sex workers in Bradford. Parts of Blamires' body were discovered on May 25th in the River Aire in Shipley. Subsequently, human tissue found in the same river was identified as belonging to Armitage. No remains of Rushworth were ever located.

On May 24, 2010, Griffiths was arrested and charged with the murders of the three women. When he appeared in the Magistrates' Court after arrest, he identified himself as "The Crossbow Cannibal." He was remanded in custody until his next court date. On June 7th, he appeared in court again by video from Wakefield Prison. A trial date of November 16, 2010 was set.

By the time Griffiths appeared in court, the body of his first victim, Susie Rushworth, had still not been found. Of his second victim, Shelley Armitage, only the shoulders, vertebrae, and connective tissue were found. Suzanne Blamires had also been dismembered, and police were only able to recover 81 fragments of her corpse.

On December 21, 2010, Griffiths pleaded guilty to all three murders and was convicted at Leeds Crown Court. Justice Openshaw sentenced him to life imprisonment with a whole-life order, ensuring he will never become eligible for parole and will likely spend the rest of his life in prison.

During his incarceration, Griffiths has attempted suicide several times. In 2011, he embarked on a 120-day hunger strike, during which he avoided contact with others.

Griffiths' prior criminal record included a three-year sentence he received at age seventeen for an unprovoked knife attack on a supermarket manager. While in custody, he expressed a desire to become a murderer, and psychiatrists warned of his fantasies about becoming a serial killer.

After a complete psychiatric exam in 1991, he was diagnosed as a "schizoid psychopath" and received a two-year prison sentence the following year for holding a knife to a girl's throat.

The police started monitoring Griffiths two years before the murders and had already confiscated hunting weapons from him. They contacted the housing association that owned Griffiths' flat after observing him reading books on dismemberment. The housing association agreed with the police's concerns and installed a better CCTV system to anticipate incidents. Despite their suspicions, the police did not have enough evidence to issue an Anti-Social Behaviour Order at the time of the murders.

In 2009, Griffiths enrolled at the University of Bradford to pursue a PhD in homicide studies. Therefore, at the time of the murders, he was a semi-professional postgraduate student in criminology.

When Griffiths was arrested and interviewed by police in 2010, he claimed to officers that he had killed a total of five sex workers in Bradford, implying there were two more victims whose deaths were unaccounted for. However, after his conviction for the three murders that year, he refused to speak to police any longer. This decision effectively prevented further investigation into any additional murders he may have committed.

One murder investigators looked into was the 2001 murder of 19-year-old **Rebecca Hall**. Her body had been found in a car park just 870 yards from Griffiths' Holmfield Court flat, where he had lived during his killing spree in 2009 and 2010. Griffiths knew Hall personally, and she was known to visit his flat regularly. Griffiths wouldn't talk to the police, but his former partner at the time disclosed that he had taken her excitedly to the place where Hall's body was found after she was discovered dead. She also mentioned that the car park was beside his doctor's surgery and pharmacy.

However, there was another suspect in Hall's murder: John Taylor, a known killer who gained notoriety after murdering schoolgirl Leanne Tiernan in 2000. The murder of Hall was one of several cold cases reopened after Taylor's conviction, and he was questioned about it as well. Evidence indicated that Hall's body had been stored for a period after her death, a known characteristic of Taylor's crimes.

DNA profiles were extracted from Hall's clothing, but the profiles were of poor quality, so they could not generate a complete profile of the unidentified individual.

In 2013, criminologist David Wilson released an episode on Griffiths in his documentary series called *Killers Behind Bars: The Untold Story*. In the episode, he linked the case of Rebecca Hall to Griffiths. Wilson also explored a possible link between Griffiths and the murder of Sheffield prostitute Dawn Shields in May 1994. However, he concluded that such a link was unlikely. The prime suspect in her murder was Alun Kyte, a multiple prostitute killer who had murdered two women in December 1993 and March 1994 and was suspected of several other murders of sex workers in England.

David Cameron, the then-new Conservative prime minister, described the murders as a "terrible shock." He suggested that the decriminalization of offenses related to prostitution should be "looked at again" but cautioned against jumping to conclusions, acknowledging the potential problems such a change could bring. Aides close to Cameron emphasized that his primary concern was addressing the social issues surrounding prostitution, including encouraging agencies to collaborate to help women leave the streets and combat drug addiction. Cameron also called for stricter measures against curb-crawling and drug abuse. The debate over whether a change in the law would protect sex workers soon became a central question.

TWENTY-ONE

Joanna Christine Dennehy

THE PETERBOROUGH DITCH MURDERS

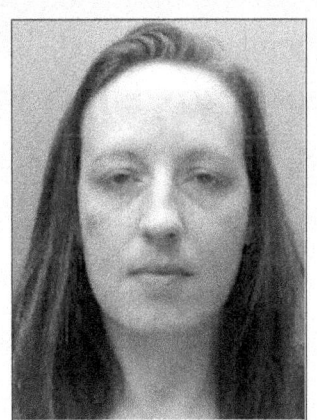

In March 2013, a series of murders that happened in Cambridgeshire, England, was dubbed "The Peterborough Ditch." All three victims were male and died from stab wounds. Their bodies were found dumped in ditches outside Peterborough. In nearby Hereford, two other men were stabbed but survived.

Joanna Christine Dennehy, a woman from Cambridgeshire, was identified as the perpetrator and was later sentenced to life imprisonment with a whole-life order. Her accomplices were Gary Stretch, who was jailed for life, with a minimum term of 19 years; Leslie Layton, who was sentenced to 14 years; and Robert Moore, who received three years.

Dennehy is only the third woman in English criminal history to be assessed as so dangerous that she can never be released. The other two to hold that notorious recognition were the "Moors Murderer" Myra Hindley and Rosemary West, for her part in a campaign of at least ten murders with her husband, Fred.

Joanna Dennehy was born in St Albans, Hertfordshire, in August 1982 and grew up near Harpenden. At the time of the killings, she was an absent mother of two young children. Dennehy only targeted men during her killing spree, expressing to an acquaintance that she did not want to kill a woman, especially not a woman with children. According to this acquaintance, Dennehy had intended to kill nine men in total, aspiring to emulate figures like Bonnie and Clyde.

Dennehy stabbed men for what she described as "entertainment," telling Gary Stretch, "I want my fun. I need you to get my fun." Later, she would tell her doctor that she found murder to be "moreish," and after the first killing, she "got a taste for it."

Victims

Lukasz Slaboszewski was her first victim. He was a Polish national who met Dennehy through a shared interest in drink and drugs. He was killed sometime around March 19, 2013. He was lured to a property in Peterborough and stabbed through the heart. His body was dumped in a wheelie bin.

John Chapman was Dennehy's housemate. Ten days after killing Slaboszewski, on March 29th, Dennehy stabbed Chapman in the neck and chest with a pocket knife. Both of their bodies were found by a passer-by around 10 miles away in a ditch at Thorney Dyke, on April 3rd.

Also, on March 29th, Dennehy killed her third victim, her landlord, boss, and lover, **Kevin Lee**.

Lee's body was found with stab wounds to the chest on March 30th near Newborough. Dennehy had dressed his body in a black sequined dress before dumping it.

After the killings, Dennehy was driven by her friend Gary Stretch (formerly known as Gary Richards) to Hereford, where she randomly stabbed two men, **Robin Bereza** and **John Rogers**, both of whom survived. After stabbing Rogers and leaving him for dead, she stole his dog. Another man, who was unwillingly traveling in the car, was later cleared of any criminal involvement in the attacks.

Arrest and Conviction

Following the killings, police launched a nationwide appeal to find Dennehy, so it wasn't long before Dennehy was found and arrested. Detective Chief Inspector Martin Brunning, from the Bedfordshire, Cambridgeshire and Hertfordshire Major Crime Unit, described her as having a "very distinctive" appearance. She was arrested in April.

In November 2013, Dennehy pleaded guilty to all three murders and two further attempted murders. Her sister Maria was unsurprised by the guilty plea, commenting, "I think she did that to control the situation. She likes people to know she's the boss."

Dennehy was held on remand at HM Prison Bronzefield. Psychiatrists later diagnosed her with psychopathic, antisocial, and borderline personality disorders.

The trial commenced at the Old Bailey in London, where Dennehy could be seen laughing during proceedings. When questioned about her decision to plead guilty, she stated, "I have pleaded guilty, and that's that." At one point during the trial, Dennehy stood up and told presiding Justice Spencer, "I don't wanna be controlled by anybody. I don't want to be controlled by my lawyers, police, or anybody."

Justice Spencer called Dennehy a "cruel, calculating, selfish, and manipulative serial killer." He sentenced her to life imprisonment with an additional order that she should never be released due to the premeditation of each murder. Spencer further described Dennehy as sadomasochistic and lacking the normal range of human emotions.

Dennehy became the third woman in the UK to be deemed "so dangerous she can never be released." The other two include Myra Hindley, the infamous killer of five children with her partner Ian Brady, and Rosemary West, who killed at least ten young women with her husband, Fred West.

Her accomplices, Gary Richards, 47, and Leslie Layton, 36, stood trial charged with various crimes relating to assisting Dennehy. Both decided not to give evidence in their defense. The jury began deliberation on February 4, 2014. Less than a week later, the jury found Richards guilty of attempted murder, and Layton was found guilty of interfering with a police investigation.

Richards and Dennehy were both sentenced to life in prison, with a minimum term of 19 years. Layton received a fourteen-year sentence, while Robert Moore, who confessed to assisting an offender, received a three-year sentence.

Aftermath

After the trial, it was revealed that Dennehy was on probation at the time of the murders. She had been given a twelve-month community order for assault and owning a dangerous dog in 2012. She had served time in prison for theft and drug offenses. She was being supervised by the Cambridgeshire and Peterborough probation service but had missed appointments. It was later determined that the staff dealing with her were inexperienced, and a more senior case manager should have been monitoring her. Nobody was reprimanded for the mistake.

During her time on remand before the trial, Dennehy was housed in segregation at HM Prison Bronzefield, a Category A prison in Surrey. Prison staff discovered an escape plot in her diary, which involved killing or seriously injuring a prison officer, cutting off one of the officer's fingers, and using the amputated finger to fool the biometric system in prison. The revelation of the plot led Dennehy to be placed in solitary confinement. She was there from September 2013, before the court proceedings, until September 2015, after the proceedings.

Dennehy later claimed that isolation left her "tearful and upset" and led to self-harm. The claim that her human rights had been violated was rejected by the High Court of Justice. Government lawyers argued that isolation was necessary due to her offenses and the risk she posed to the public if she escaped. Justice Singh found that solitary confinement was "following law (...) at all material times it has been necessary and proportionate."

After her trial, Dennehy was returned to HMP Bronzefield. In 2018, she requested permission to marry her cellmate Hayley Palmer. The engagement caused concern among Palmer's family, who feared Dennehy might pose a danger to her safety. That same year, both Dennehy and Palmer attempted suicide during a suicide pact.

By June 2020, Dennehy was reported to be in a relationship with another prisoner, twenty-five-year-old Emma Aitken, serving a twelve-year sentence for her part in a murder case where the victim's body was dumped outside a social club.

In 2019, Dennehy was transferred to Low Newton Prison in County Durham. Upon her arrival, there were allegations that she threatened to kill Rosemary West, who was subsequently moved to another prison. However, the government denied this allegation.

In May 2021, it was again reported that Dennehy and Hayley Palmer, who were back together after Aitken had been released, intended to marry. Palmer was released after serving her sixteen-year sentence.

TWENTY-TWO

Lisa Letby

L ucy Letby was a former British nurse who was convicted of murdering seven babies and attempting to murder six others between 2015 and 2016. Letby came under suspicion due to a high number of infant deaths occurring at the neonatal unit of the Countess of Chester Hospital shortly after she began working there.

Letby was arrested and charged in November 2020 with eight counts of murder and ten counts of attempted murder, where she pleaded not guilty and maintained her innocence during a subsequent Nursing and Midwifery Council disciplinary panel. During her trial, it was revealed that she injected the infants with air or insulin, overfed them, physically abused them with medical tools, removed over 250 confidential nursing handover sheets, and falsified patient records to avoid suspicion.

On August 21, 2023, Letby was sentenced to life imprisonment with a whole-life order. In February 2024, she renewed an application to appeal her conviction, which the Court of Appeal heard in April of that year and reserved judgment for later. Letby faces a retrial in June 2024 on a single charge that resulted in a hung jury in the original trial.

Letby is considered the most prolific serial child killer in modern British history. The Cheshire Constabulary suspects she may have additional victims at Liverpool Women's Hospital, where two infants died during her training. Management at the Countess of Chester Hospital faced criticism for ignoring warnings about Letby that could have prevented some of the killings. In response, the British government has commissioned an independent statutory inquiry into the circumstances surrounding the murders.

Lucy Letby was born in Hereford, Herefordshire, on January 4, 1990. She was the only child of a finance manager and an accounts clerk. She attended Aylestone School and Hereford Sixth Form College. According to a friend who has known her since secondary school, Letby's mother had a difficult birth, and Lucy often spoke of how deeply grateful she was to the nurses who helped save her life, so much so that it inspired her to pursue a career in nursing.

Letby studied nursing education at the University of Chester, where she worked as a student nurse during her three years of training. She completed placements at Liverpool Women's Hospital and the Countess of Chester Hospital. Letby was the first member of her family to attend university and successfully graduated in September 2011.

After graduation in 2012, Letby began her

nursing career at the Countess of Chester Hospital neonatal unit. Her duties included caring for many babies with varying support needs. She seemed happy at her new job and often expressed joy in seeing the babies progress, including supporting their families. Letby also actively worked to raise funds for a new neonatal unit to be built at the hospital. Her colleagues mentioned that Letby found non-intensive care work boring.

During the training stage of her career, Letby had two placements at Liverpool Women's Hospital in late 2012 and early 2015. Once the second one was completed in 2015, she qualified to work with infants in intensive care at Countess of Chester Hospital.

From June 2015 to June 2016, a series of troubling incidents occurred at the hospital's neonatology unit. During this period, four collapses were reported, resulting in three deaths. Typically, the unit experienced only two or three deaths annually, and the infants failed to respond generally to resuscitation efforts.

Due to growing concerns about the higher-than-normal infant mortality rate, a ward manager conducted a review and noted that Letby was the only staff member present at all incidents. At the time, she was one of the few qualified junior nurses on the unit and often covered extra shifts due to staffing shortages. The concerns were relayed to the lead neonatologist and then to those higher in management. However, because of staffing shortages, they were ignored. The only thing that could be done was to reassign Letby from night to day shifts, which happened in April 2016. The deaths continued but now occurred during the day, again when Letby was on duty.

The neonatologist and medical consultants asked management to remove Letby from clinical duties pending an investigation into her conduct. Urgent meetings were requested with hospital management, but the executive team attributed the spike in deaths to coincidence and took no substantial action. Reports from the nationwide MBRRACE-UK project highlighted a neonatal death rate at least 10% higher than expected, with the total in 2015 doubling that of the previous year.

Then, in June 2016, following the deaths of two triplet babies, medical consultants raised concerns that could no longer be ignored. But the duty executive insisted she was safe to work. By late June, the trust's executive directors convened and decided against involving the police, concerned about the hospital's reputation.

Instead, they organized a limited review through the Royal College of Paediatrics and Child Health (RCPCH), which commenced in September 2016. In the meantime, Letby was transferred to the patient experience team in July of that year and later to the risk and patient safety office, where she worked until her arrest in 2018.

The RCPCH's review excluded investigating Letby's actions or the deaths directly. Instead, it focused on the unit's general service. Despite recommendations for a detailed case review of each death, a thorough external independent or forensic review was not conducted. The medical director's misleading presentation to the hospital board further exacerbated the situation.

In September 2016, Letby lodged a formal grievance about her transfer from clinical duties. It was upheld in January 2017, citing orchestrated actions without hard evidence. The trust supported her return to the neonatal unit and offered her opportunities for further development.

In March 2017, medical consultants sought police involvement. They met with Cheshire Constabulary in April 2017, and "Operation Hummingbird" commenced to investigate the incidents. Initially exploring various hypotheses, including natural causes and organic reasons, the investigation eventually considered the possibility of inflicted harm.

Finally, in July 2018, Letby was arrested by police and brought in for questioning as a possible suspect in eight murders and six attempted murders. Following her arrest, authorities began scrutinizing her entire career, including her time at Liverpool Women's Hospital. Letby was released on bail initially on July 6, 2018, but was rearrested on June 10, 2019, and bailed again on June 13th that year.

On November 10, 2020, she was arrested again and denied bail. Letby has consistently denied all charges against her, attributing the deaths to issues with hospital hygiene and staffing levels.

Trial

Letby's trial commenced with Justice Goss at Manchester Crown Court on October 10, 2022. Letby pleaded not guilty to seven counts of murder and 15 counts of attempted murder. Families of the victims, as well as Letby's parents, were present throughout the trial.

The child victims were identified in court as Child A to Child Q. The media was strictly prohibited from identifying the seventeen babies and the nine colleagues who gave evidence, a level of secrecy rarely seen outside matters of national security. The names of the living victims were also protected until their 18th birthdays, as ordered by Justice Steyn two years before the trial. Several witnesses requested anonymity, including a doctor whom Letby was reportedly infatuated. The judge approved, emphasizing the importance of their testimony over their public identification.

The mother of one victim recounted hearing her infant scream and finding him with blood around his mouth. Letby was present in the room. She allegedly explained the blood as coming from a nasogastric tube, stating, "Trust me, I'm a nurse." The baby's condition deteriorated rapidly, and he later died in his parents' arms.

Shockingly, following the infant's death, Letby sent a sympathy card to the parents on the day of the baby's funeral. It was later discovered that Letby had taken photos of the card before sending it and kept these images on her phone. During the trial, it was revealed that Letby had to be told multiple times not to enter a room where the grieving parents of another victim were present. She also confided in a colleague that taking Child

A to the mortuary had been "the hardest thing she ever had to do."

The Crown Prosecution Service presented evidence of letters and texts from Letby sent to friends, describing them as a "live blogging" of events and displaying "intrusive curiosity." For example, shortly after the collapse of Child M, Letby sent texts celebrating a gambling win and making plans for a party. It was also revealed that Letby had looked up several Facebook profiles of the victim's parents, especially on the anniversary of a baby's death.

The prosecution argued that suspicious incidents began in 2015 when Letby became qualified to work with infants in intensive care. They highlighted a series of incidents, including cases where infants unexpectedly collapsed while under Letby's care. These incidents included the case of a desaturating infant with whom Letby allegedly failed to intervene, claiming the infant had just begun to decline.

In one of the more concerning cases, twins collapsed within 24 hours of each other under Letby's care, with one dying and the other becoming seriously ill. Laboratory analysis later confirmed that the deceased twin had been deliberately poisoned with insulin, which had not been prescribed. It was suspected that Letby had injected air into the bloodstream of the surviving twin.

Witnesses testified that concerns about Letby had been raised with hospital administration before her arrest but were dismissed. Despite recommendations to remove Letby from duty after multiple incidents, the hospital administration refused, leading to further incidents under her care.

Letby was the only staff member present for all 25 suspicious incidents. No further suspicious incidents occurred after her removal from duty, and the unit was downgraded.

During the trial, it was also revealed that Letby had falsified patient records, altering the times of collapses to distance herself from the crimes. Criminal psychologist Dr. David Holmes noted that the methods Letby employed, such as injecting insulin and air and overfeeding milk, were chosen specifically to evade detection.

Overall, the prosecution presented a pattern of suspicious incidents under Letby's care, suggesting deliberate actions to harm infants, which Letby denied throughout the trial. Searches of Letby's and her parents' homes and her handbag uncovered a series of handwritten

Post-it notes authored by Letby. Among these were fragmentary phrases such as "Help," "I'm sorry that you couldn't have a chance at life," "I don't want to do this anymore," "Not good enough," and "Why me?" "I haven't done anything wrong," "We tried our best, and it wasn't enough," "I am evil, I did this," and "I killed them on purpose because I'm not good enough to care for them." The defense argued that these notes were just the overreaction of a young woman in fear and despair while facing discipline for a grievance procedure with the NHS Trust. In contrast, the prosecution contended that the notes reflected Letby's frustration at being removed from the neonatal unit.

Letby herself denied that the notes were a confession, describing them as a reflection of her mental turmoil during the investigation. The *Guardian*, reporting after the trial, described the notes as "the closest the prosecution had to a confession." The *Telegraph* highlighted one note that read, "I'll never marry or have children, I'll never know what it's like to have a family," suggesting that Letby's fear of not having her own children might have been a motivation for the killings. Additionally, Letby's diary was discovered to be marked with the initials of the deceased babies on the exact days they died.

During searches of Letby's home, investigators found sensitive medical documents hidden under her bed, including nursing handover sheets, resuscitation records, and blood gas readings. Among the 257 sheets discovered, 21 were related to infants Letby was accused of harming. Letby testified that she had a habit of collecting paper and had forgotten to remove the sheets from her pockets at the hospital. She claimed she could not destroy them, although a paper shredder was found in her home.

In May 2023, Letby testified in court, breaking down in tears and stating that she felt incompetent but insisted she "meant no harm." She described how the allegations had severely affected her mental health, saying, "I don't think you can be accused of anything worse than that. I just changed as a person, and my mental health deteriorated. I felt isolated from my friends on the unit." She frequently contradicted herself, muddled her story, and grew increasingly frustrated with the prosecution's questioning, which contrasted with her usual calm demeanor.

Letby's defense lawyer argued that she was "a dedicated nurse in a system which has failed" and criticized the prosecution's case based on the assumption of deliberate harm combined with the coincidence of Letby's presence on certain occasions. Essentially, they were saying that the issues in the neonatal unit were far too significant to be blamed on one person. They suggested that with one of the baby boys thought to have been murdered by Letby, the extraordinary bleeding could have been caused by a rigid wire or tube. The prosecution also tried to suggest that the use of insulin was a therapeutic measure, but Letby's colleagues denied any therapeutic use of insulin.

After the jury delivered their final verdicts on August 18, 2023, Lucy Letby was found guilty of seven counts of murder for killing seven babies. She murdered them by using several different means, including overfeeding, injecting them with insulin to poison them, injecting them with air, and assaulting them with medical tools.

Additionally, Letby was found guilty of seven counts of attempted murder involving six infants. She was acquitted on two counts of attempted murder, while the jury could not reach verdicts on six attempted murder charges. The prosecution requested twenty-eight days to consider seeking a retrial for these counts.

On August 21, 2023, Letby was sentenced to

the most severe sentence under English law—to serve life with no possibility of parole. Letby is the fourth woman in UK legal history to receive such a sentence. Justice Goss said that Letby's murders were a cruel, well-planned campaign of child murder involving the smallest and most vulnerable of children. He emphasized the absence of remorse, citing "deep malevolence bordering on sadism" and declaring the offenses merited a whole life order due to their severity.

Letby chose not to attend the sentencing hearing and did not hear the victim impact statements read out or her sentence delivered. In response, Secretary of State for Justice Alex Chalk pledged that the government would explore legislative changes to compel defendants to attend their sentencing. Prime Minister Rishi Sunak announced on August 30, 2023, that legislation would be introduced to Parliament to enforce the attendance of convicted criminals at their sentencing hearings, potentially using force.

Following the trial, Letby was transferred to HMP Low Newton, a closed prison for women in County Durham. As of January 2024, she remains incarcerated at HM Prison Bronzefield.

Aftermath

Letby was placed on an interim suspension from the Nursing and Midwifery Council on March 13, 2020, while out on bail, but by December 2023, she was completely removed from the nursing registry. She responded by saying she didn't accept any guilt but didn't contest her removal.

In January 2024, Letby applied to the Court of Appeal for permission to appeal her convictions, which a judge refused. Letby renewed her application in February 2024. Following a three-day hearing in April 2024, three judges of the Court of Appeal reserved judgment. Their written decision on whether to grant permission will be issued later.

During a hearing on September 25, 2023, the CPS confirmed that there would be a retrial on one of the six counts of attempted murder against Letby—the one on which the jury at the original trial could not reach a verdict. A trial date of June 10, 2024, has been set, pending the judge's decision on Letby's appeal against her existing convictions.

Following the verdict, it was reported that police were investigating whether Letby harmed other babies. There is an ongoing investigation into incidents that detectives have identified as "suspicious" at the Countess of Chester Hospital, involving approximately 30 other infants. Neonatologists have reviewed about 4,000 admissions at both the hospital and Liverpool Women's Hospital, where Letby worked from 2012 to 2015, and any cases of "unexpected and unexplained" deteriorations are being passed on to the police. Police informed at least one family that their child's birth at the latter hospital was part of the investigation. Cheshire Police have stated that further charges could "possibly" be brought against Letby due to these ongoing investigations.

Slater and Gordon, a law firm representing two of the victims' families, issued a statement calling for the inquiry to have the power to compel witnesses to participate. The statement argued that a non-statutory hearing "must rely on the goodwill of those involved to share their testimony."

Education Minister Gillian Keegan mentioned that the inquiry type would be reviewed after the chair was appointed. On August 30, 2023, Health

Secretary Steve Barclay announced that the inquiry had been upgraded to a statutory inquiry, describing it as the best way forward, which would compel witnesses to give evidence. Justice Thirlwall was appointed to chair the inquiry. The inquiry's terms of reference were published on October 19, 2023, and updated on November 22, 2023, when she formally opened the investigation.

The British Medical Association, representing doctors, urged a process to hold NHS managers and healthcare administrators accountable for mismanagement, akin to how the General Medical Council can strike off doctors who harm patients. The neonatal consultant, who had raised concerns with administrators about Letby, also called for regulating healthcare management.

Despite Letby's conviction, many of her friends and former colleagues still believe in her innocence. Speculative theories questioning the outcome circulated on the internet. The case has attracted amateur investigators who suspect a miscarriage of justice.

Statistician Richard D. Gill and lawyer Neil Mackenzie KC, who co-authored a work on using statistics in court cases, have also raised concerns about the outcome. In May 2024, The *New Yorker* published a feature article by staff writer Rachel Aviv that questioned Letby's conviction. Aviv reported that pervasive staffing shortages at Countess of Chester Hospital's neonatal unit had significantly increased poor care outcomes during and after Letby's tenure. She criticized the prosecution for using flawed statistical reasoning, emphasizing events that supported their theory while discounting contradictory evidence, which she described as an example of the "Texas sharpshooter fallacy," an incorrect argument committed when differences in data are ignored but similarities are overemphasized.

In the article, Aviv also questioned the testimony of Dewi Evans, a retired consultant pediatrician and prosecution witness, whose attestation formed a vital part of the case. In the past, a Court of Appeals judge had criticized Evans for his opinions being worthless and outside his professional competence. Due to reporting restrictions related to Letby's pending retrial, the online version of *The New Yorker* article was disabled for British readers. Still, the print edition was available on British newsstands as usual.

Dewi Evans has called for an investigation into

the possibility of corporate manslaughter charges related to the Letby case. He has claimed to have received abuse from Letby's supporters online, who doubt the legitimacy of her conviction. He described the abuse as being similar to the intimidation received from supporters of outed abusers in the 1980s and 1990s. He claims that people find it difficult to accept that a killer could be a "young, white, English nurse from a respectable background" who "hid in plain sight," adding: "It is crucial to their getting away with it that they appear normal."

The Royal College of Paediatrics and Child Health stated, "We must learn from these crimes and how Lucy Letby was able to bring harm to these babies so that no situation like this can ever happen again," and welcomed the independent inquiry.

It was reported that the British government is examining how Letby's pension can be stopped. The NHS pension scheme regulations provide for a forfeit of pensions after a conviction of certain crimes.

Motive

The prosecution in Letby's case suggested that boredom, thrill-seeking, and a desire to "Play God" were potential motives for the killings. They also alleged that Letby had a secret relationship with a married doctor who was involved in some of the cases. As evidence, they pointed to Letby's frequent texts during specific night shifts telling him that she trusted him with everything and loved him and that he was her best friend and needed help. Letby denied all these claims, including any suggestion of a relationship or crush on the doctor.

A former detective who led the investigation into the 1990s Beverley Allitt's case drew parallels between Allitt's and Letby's cases. He suggested that Letby might have mimicked Allitt's methods. Then, Criminal Psychologists Dominic Wilmott and David Holmes proposed that Letby may have been motivated by "factitious disorder imposed on another," a theory suggested in Allitt's case. The mental disorder was also known as "fabricated or induced illness by carers" (FII) and was first named "Munchausen syndrome by proxy" (MSbP) or "Munchausen Syndrome."

Emeritus Professor of Criminology David Wilson published an opinion piece in *The Guardian* in August 2023, speculating that Letby was driven by a "hero complex." Later that month, Wilson discussed Letby on *Newsnight*, arguing that healthcare killers often enter the profession to target vulnerable victims, such as the very old or very young.

TWENTY-THREE

Stephen Akinmurele

THE CUL-DE-SAC KILLER

S tephen Akinmurele, a.k.a. "The Cul-de-sac Killer," was a suspected serial killer charged with murdering five elderly individuals between 1995 and 1998: Eric and Joan Boardman, Jemmimah Cargill, Dorothy Harris, and Marjorie Ashton. Akinmurele was a suspected serial killer because just weeks before his trial, he killed himself in Manchester prison.

Stephen Oladimeji K. Akinmurele was born in Nigeria to a Nigerian father and a white British mother. In 1988, he and his mother moved back to England, the Isle of Man, before relocating to Blackpool, where he worked as a barman.

Akinmurele had a history of mental illness and began committing crimes against the elderly at age eleven. He was reportedly drawn to situations involving older adults, with police suggesting he had an intense hatred towards old people and derived pleasure from killing them. His victims were all senior citizens. He was dubbed the "cul-de-sac killer" because his victims were all older and living in quiet suburban areas.

Akinmurele's first two known victims were seventy-seven-year-old **Eric Boardman** and his wife, seventy-four-year-old **Joan Boardman**. The couple lived in Blackpool and were murdered there on October 30, 1998, and discovered by their daughter. Eric was found under a wardrobe in the hallway and had been beaten to death, while Joan, who had been strangled, was left on the living room floor. Akinmurele used a homemade club using batteries that was found beneath Eric's body. He was arrested and charged with their murders on November 1, 1998.

In the months following his arrest, Akinmurele was charged with three additional murders. In November 1998, he was accused of the murder of **Jemmimah Cargill**, 75, his former landlady, who died in a flat fire in October 1998, just before the Boardman murders.

After a joint investigation between Lancashire and Manx police, Akinmurele was charged with two murders, sixty-eight-year-old **Dorothy Harris** and seventy-two-year-old **Marjorie Ashton**, both from the Isle of Man. Dorothy Harris, who was partially blind and deaf, was killed in February 1996. Marjorie Ashton was found strangled in her home in Ballasalla in May 1995.

Detectives believed that Akinmurele might have been responsible for additional deaths, so they re-examined other house fires and sudden deaths in the area. While in custody, Akinmurele confessed to three more murders, including that of a wanderer on the Isle of Man. He claimed to have murdered the man and buried his body on a cliff overlooking the sea. Although Manx police found a gun with his fingerprint on it, they did not find a body despite extensive excavation. Police believe that Akinmurele made these false confessions to conceal his true motivation for the murders, which was his hatred for older adults.

Akinmurele committed suicide in Manchester Prison in August 1999, just weeks before his trial. He hanged himself from a window using a ligature. His girlfriend had warned the correctional officers that he wanted to kill himself and had tried to commit suicide twice before. A suicide note was found in his pocket after his death. In the note, Akinmurele wrote, "I know it's not right to always think like this, but it's always on my mind. I can't help the way I feel. I know what I did was wrong, and I feel for them, but it doesn't mean I won't do it again. I'll keep feeling mad because I can't take any more of this, and that's why I'm saying goodbye." He also wrote to his mother, stating, "I couldn't take any more of the feeling like how I do now, always wanting to kill."

TWENTY-FOUR

John Duffy and David Mulcahy

THE RAILWAY KILLERS

J ohn Francis Duffy and David Mulcahy are two British serial rapists and killers who attacked several women and children at railway stations during the 1980s in the southern part of England. Their crimes are often called "The Railway Murders," and they are frequently referred to as the "Railway Rapists" or the "Railway Killers." After Duffy was identified, the press dubbed him the "Railway Murderer" or "Laser Eyes.'

Duffy was born in 1958, and Mulcahy in 1959. They were lifelong friends and inseparable since their days at Haverstock School in North London. They were both expelled from the school when a teacher found them laughing and covered in blood after beating a hedgehog to death.

Crimes

The 1982 attacks on two women near Hampstead and Barnes Train Stations marked the beginning of a series of assaults and sexual assaults on a total of twenty women near railway stations in Northern London. Most of these attacks occurred late at night in secluded areas near various railway stations in northern London, particularly near Hampstead and Barnes stations. Further assaults took place in 1984, and in 1985, three women were raped on the same night in Hendon.

The Metropolitan Police in West London launched an urgent investigation, "Operation Hart," to apprehend the perpetrators. The women described one attacker as a short, ginger-haired man and the second as a more prominent man. DNA was unavailable then, but some suspects were eliminated because of their blood type.

Victims

Nineteen-year-old **Alison Day** was heading to meet her boyfriend at his workplace on a desolate trading estate near Hackney Wick Station on December 29, 1985. After driving around several train stations without having any luck finding their next victim, Duffy and Mulcahy suddenly spotted Day leaving Hackney Wick Station. They watched as she made a phone call at a telephone booth, and after she finished, they decided to follow her. Walking down an alley towards the canal, she met up with Duffy and Mulcahy.

Duffy threatened her with a knife, and both men sexually assaulted her. They then forced her to walk across live railway lines to a bridge parapet. Day fell from the bridge into the canal but managed to swim to the bank. Duffy and Mulcahy pulled her from the water and took her to a wasteland, where they strangled her to death with her blouse. Her coat pockets were weighted with cobbles stones and sunk into the River Lea. After her body was found, the Metropolitan Police in east London launched a separate investigation,

"Operation Lea." Following Day's murder, the press nicknamed her attacker the "Railway Rapist."

The subsequent murder of fifteen-year-old Dutch schoolgirl **Maartje Tamboezer** in West Horsley, Surrey, on the afternoon of April 17, 1986, changed the moniker to "The Railway Killer." Tamboezer was knocked from her bicycle with a wire strung between two trees. They raped, strangled, and set her body on fire.

The Surrey Police initiated "Operation Bluebell," while Detective Superintendent Charles Farquhar, an experienced east London murder investigator, took over the Day murder investigation. He linked Day's murder with the previous railway rapes and then with Tamboezer's murder, noting similarities such as the use of a tourniquet ligature made from a belt and twig.

About a month later, on May 18, 1986, twenty-nine-year-old **Anne Lock** was on her way to work, and when she got off the train at Brookmans Park in Hertfordshire, sometime after leaving the station, she was abducted and killed.

Duffy, a martial arts expert and former railway carpenter, was suspected when Detective Superintendent John Hurst remembered him. Duffy was known to the police due to a prior charge of raping his estranged wife. He Hurst recalled Duffy holding the belief that rape was a "natural male instinct."

When searching Duffy's parents' house, a rare type of string called "somyarn" was found, linking him to the second murder victim. She had been strangled using an unusual method that he knew of from his former job.

Mulcahy, Duffy's close friend, was also questioned. However, the victims were unable to identify him in a police lineup, which at the time required the victim to get close enough to touch the offender physically. Mulcahy was released due to lack of evidence.

Detectives asked David Canter, a psychologist from the University of Surrey specializing in geographical psychology, to help them with the case. This was the first use of "psychological offender profiling" in Britain. Canter analyzed the details of each crime and developed a profile of the attacker's personality, habits, and traits. Despite this effort, another attack occurred before they could make an arrest. A fourteen-year-old girl was raped in a park. The last attack prompted Canter to pioneer investigative psychology.

In addition to their joint crimes, Duffy began committing rapes on his own. He was arrested on November 26, 1986, while following a woman in a secluded park. Evidence linking him to the Tamboezer murder was discovered, and rape victims were able to identify him positively.

Duffy was charged with three murders and several rapes. During questioning, he refused to disclose his accomplice's identity. Mulcahy was arrested as a suspect, though insufficient evidence prevented his charges.

On February 1988, Duffy went to trial and was convicted of two murders and four rapes. He was acquitted of the rape and murder of Anne Lock, as her body was not found until weeks after her murder, making forensic evidence inconclusive.

The judge sentenced him to a minimum of thirty years, and the Home Secretary extended it to a whole life term. Duffy chose not to appeal his sentence, later expressing regret for his crimes and acknowledging that the conviction was justified.

Aftermath

After the trial, much attention was given to David Canter's psychological profile. Duffy matched 13 of the 17 characteristics Canter was able to predict about the attacker's lifestyle and habits. This profiling method subsequently became standard practice in policing.

After his conviction, Duffy disclosed to a forensic psychologist what the police already knew: that he had not acted alone in the attacks on women. However, at that time, he did not provide any further details.

Les Bolland, a junior police officer during the initial investigation and trial in 1988, remained interested in the case and, by March 1995, had risen to a position where he could initiate or advance an inquiry. John Duffy agreed to be interviewed by Bolland but warned that it would take time. The inquiry led to a series of visits, and eventually, Duffy requested assistance from the prison psychological service.

In late 1997, a new psychologist began working at the prison. Bolland informed her that progress could be made if Duffy received counseling, which was arranged. By June 1998,

Duffy agreed to start making whole, detailed admissions to the police.

Due to difficulties conducting interviews in prison, Duffy was secretly transported to a remote police station in Hertfordshire for a week. The week chosen coincided with the football World Cup. Duffy asked for the interviews to be scheduled around the matches, which Bolland, a football fan himself, agreed to.

The interviews were conducted under police caution, meaning he must admit guilt. Although Duffy was not legally in jeopardy, they were taped. He confessed to several rapes but initially claimed he could remember no more. Additional cases from police records were presented to jog his memory, and he recalled further incidents. Duffy was explicit that these crimes were committed with his friend David Mulcahy.

Eventually, Duffy admitted to all of his offenses, including the three murders committed with Mulcahy. He provided detailed explanations of what had happened to Anne Lock. Duffy told Bolland that a Michael Jackson song called "Thriller" had played a role in psyching them up before attacks—Mulcahy's house contained the tape.

Duffy also explained how their approach to

and control over victims evolved, describing them as "shockingly skilled" in Bolland's words.

Duffy spoke calmly and matter-of-factly, except when discussing the Tamboezer murder.

Nine months after the interview series, Duffy faced seventeen charges of rape and conspiracy to rape. He admitted guilt to all, asserting he had done so with Mulcahy. Despite being found not guilty of murdering Anne Lock, he was charged with her rape. In March 1999, Duffy appeared in court and confessed to all seventeen charges.

Following Duffy's revelations, Mulcahy, a married father of four, was surveilled by police for several months before being arrested in February 1999. DNA tests, unavailable during the original investigation, conclusively proved his involvement, supported by evidence found during a search of his home. Mulcahy chose not to answer any questions during interviews. By this time, Mulcahy had already acquired a criminal record as he had been convicted of assault and battery for beating one of his sons, receiving a non-custodial sentence.

Duffy was scheduled to appear as a prosecution witness at Mulcahy's trial. Mulcahy's defense team sent letters to prisoners on Duffy's wing, claiming lawyer-client privilege, telling them that Duffy would be a witness for the prosecution against Mulcahy. They warned that if Duffy testified, a miscarriage of justice would occur, placing Duffy in clear danger. Prison authorities took action to protect him. A complaint to the solicitors revealed that a clerical worker's letters were an error, sent to prisoners who were not their clients.

Mulcahy's trial commenced on September 11, 2000, and Les Bolland, an important witness, was accused of conspiring to persuade Duffy to give false evidence against Mulcahy. Over two weeks, Duffy appeared as a prosecution witness and provided detailed evidence. This trial marked the first time a Category A prisoner testified against an accomplice.

Prosecution evidence presented Mulcahy as the primary perpetrator, the first to decide that sexual stimulation was insufficient and that murder was required for satisfaction. Described as "smug and arrogant" in court, Mulcahy denied all allegations, claiming that Duffy was lying, police had planted the DNA evidence, and a fingerprint on the tape used during a rape was not his. The defense sought to have Mulcahy's interview tapes from the 1980s excluded from evidence.

After being convicted of three counts of

murder and seven counts of rape, Mulcahy was sentenced to three life sentences with a 30-year recommendation and 24 years imprisonment for each rape offense. However, he was not given a whole-life tariff, as politically set tariffs had been barred when his case was due for review.

A few weeks later, Duffy, who was already serving a complete life sentence, was sentenced to twelve years imprisonment for each of the seven rapes he had confessed to.

Neither man is expected ever to be released from prison. David Mulcahy maintains his innocence and has a website copyrighted under his name since 2011, advocating for a retrial.

Following Mulcahy's conviction, police reopened hundreds of unsolved sexual assaults and murders throughout the country, suspecting that the two men may have committed more offenses than Duffy confessed to. Detective Superintendent Andy Murphy suspected that Mulcahy had committed further acts of violence against women alone and with Duffy, urging any surviving victims to come forward. Neither man was ever charged with any additional crimes.

Sources

1. "Murder, Mental Illness, and the Question of Nursing 'Character' in Early Twentieth Century England" | *History Workshop Journal* | Oxford Academic (oup.com)
2. Furio, Jennifer: "Team Killers: A Comparative Study of Collaborative Criminals" Google Books
3. Sach and Walters – The History Room (history-room.co.uk)
4. "Mt A drama presents *The Drowning Girls*, an accurate crime tale that centers female voices" *CHMA*
5. Rose, Andrew: *Lethal Witness*, Sutton Publishing 2007, Kent State University Press 2009
6. Moore, James: *Murder by Numbers: Fascinating Figures Behind The World's Worst Crimes*. History Press. 2018. p. 18. ISBN: 9780750981453.
7. February 22, 1942, "A 'Ripper' stalked in the blackout" *Trove* (nla.gov.au)
8. Bob Higgins (telegraph.co.uk)
9. PressReader.com - Digital Newspaper & Magazine Subscriptions
10. Cummins, "Serial Blackout Killer in UK," *The Leader-Post*, June 25, 1942, *Newspapers.com*
11. Church, Mabel: *Unsolved Murder 1941*, 225 Hampstead Road, London, Unsolved Mysteries UK (unsolved-murders.co.uk)
12. *PressReader.com* - Digital Newspaper & Magazine Subscriptions
13. September 29, 1951 "Clue of the Air Force Gas Mask," *Trove* (nla.gov.au)

14. February 17, 1942 "MAN CHARGED WITH MURDER OF 3 WOMEN," *Trove* (nla.gov.au)

15. British Executions - Execution of Gordon Frederick Cummins - 1942 murder - Capital Punishment

16. https://www.biography.com/crime/graham-young

17. https://onlinelibrary.wiley.com/doi/abs/10.1002/cbm.132

18. https://www.theguardian.com/artanddesign/2009/mar/02/art-ukcrime?keepThis=true&TB_iframe=true&height=650&width=850

19. Brabin, Daniel: Rillington Place 1999 ISBN 978-0-11-702417-5

20. Dawson, Kate Winkler: *Death in the Air: The True Story of a Serial Killer*, The Great London Smog, and the Strangling of a City 2017 ISBN 978-0-316-50686-1

21. https://web.archive.org/web/20110714172341/http://www.newcriminologist.com/article.asp?nid=1120

22. Honeycombe, Gordon: *The Murders of the Black Museum 1870–1970*. ISBN 978-1-854-71160-1. 1982.

23. https://web.archive.org/web/20210808003833/https://www.oldpolicecellsmuseum.org.uk/content/history/sussex_murders/john_george_haigh

24. https://trove.nla.gov.au/newspaper/article/130252539

25. https://search.worldcat.org/title/222592555

26. https://www.bbc.co.uk/news/world-16242235

27. https://www.yorkshirepost.co.uk/news/black-panther-neilson-died-from-pneumonia-inquest-told-1913031

28. http://news.bbc.co.uk/local/shropshire/hi/people_and_places/history/newsid_8365000/8365884.stm
29. https://www.birminghammail.co.uk/news/midlands-news/black-panther-donald-neilsons-trail-8464470
30. https://www.hulldailymail.co.uk/news/hull-east-yorkshire-news/hulls-worst-serial-killer-bruce-6621713
31. https://galeapps.gale.com/apps/auth?userGroupName=corlonli&origURL=https%3A%2F%2Fgo.gale.com%2Fps%2Fi.do%3Fp%3DTTDA%26u%3Dcorlonli%26id%3DGALE%7CCS85296526%26v%3D2.1%26it%3Dr&prodId=TTDA
32. https://www.itv.com/news/calendar/2022-02-08/serial-arsonist-bruce-lee-loses-appeal-over-string-of-fatal-fires-in-1970s
33. https://www.bbc.com/news/uk-england-humber-58876813
34. https://web.archive.org/web/20181019135453/https://www.yorkshirepost.co.uk/news/analysis/a-city-s-memories-branded-in-fire-of-killer-s-reign-of-terror-30-years-ago-1-2314856
35. https://www.kentonline.co.uk/dartford/news/killer-denied-release-for-death-of-kent-priest-247216/
36. https://web.archive.org/web/20080401002015/http://www.crimelibrary.com/notorious_murders/mass/patrick_mackay/2.html
37. Fred Dinenage Murder Casebook
38. www.pressreader.com/uk/the-sunday-telegraph/20190616/281754155838005

39. https://webarchive.nationalarchives.gov.uk/
    ukgwa/20110204013216/http://www.
    hmcourts-service.gov.uk/cms/144_12952.htm
40. http://news.bbc.co.uk/2/hi/uk_news/england/
    8149050.stm
41. https://books.google.ca/books?id=
    DwNVbOcTncwC&pg=PA68&redir_esc=y#v=
    onepage&q&f=false
42. https://www.bbc.co.uk/news/uk-england-tyne-
    24637209
43. https://www.independent.co.uk/news/uk/killer-
    did-not-target-school-head-says-1441299.html
44. http://news.bbc.co.uk/2/hi/uk_news/england/
    wear/3839469.stm
45. https://www.bbc.com/news/uk-england-tyne-
    41525383
46. https://www.upi.com/Archives/1993/05/28/
    Killer-nurse-gets-13-life-sentences-in-Britain/
    1050738561600/
47. https://web.archive.org/web/
    20070208092708/http://www.crimelibrary.
    com/notorious_murders/angels/beverly_allitt/
    6.html
48. https://www.independent.co.uk/news/uk/
    drawn-curtains-in-a-silent-village-the-beverly-
    allitt-case-on-friday-this-baby-killer-will-be-
    sentenced-for-26-attacks-including-four-murders-
    what-do-they-make-of-it-all-back-home-
    2324732.html
49. https://www.independent.co.uk/news/uk/
    warning-signs-about-allitt-overlooked-
    1391435.html
50. http://news.bbc.co.uk/2/hi/uk_news/england/
    lincolnshire/7130211.stm

51. https://www.independent.co.uk/news/uk/fleet-street-s-perverse-cocktail-of-kinky-sex-and-a-serial-killer-neil-mckenna-berates-the-reporting-of-a-series-of-homosexual-murders-1492873.html

52. https://www.independent.co.uk/news/uk/calculating-murderer-who-preyed-on-gays-terry-kirby-builds-up-a-picture-of-a-man-with-a-lethal-wish-to-prove-he-was-someone-of-consequence-1468747.html

53. https://www.theguardian.com/uk/2007/may/15/gayrights.ukcrime

54. https://www.bbc.com/news/uk-england-17117441

55. https://www.radiotimes.com/programme/b-idbqiu/britains-most-evil-killers-season-3/

56. https://www.bbc.com/news/uk-england-35539761

57. http://news.bbc.co.uk/2/hi/uk_news/england/london/7227830.stm

58. https://www.bbc.com/news/uk-england-13875507

59. http://news.bbc.co.uk/2/hi/uk_news/england/surrey/7268759.stm

60. https://www.theguardian.com/uk/2011/jun/24/levi-bellfield-profile-milly-dowler

61. https://www.scotsman.com/news/the-hatred-that-turned-colin-norris-into-serial-killer-2478080

62. https://www.telegraph.co.uk/news/uknews/1580549/Colin-Norris-From-student-to-deadly-abuser.html

63. http://news.bbc.co.uk/2/hi/uk_news/england/7268836.stm

64. https://web.archive.org/web/
    20080315010951/http://www.telegraph.co.uk/
    news/main.jhtml?xml=%2Fnews%2F2008%
    2F03%2F03%2Fnnurse503.xml
65. https://www.chroniclelive.co.uk/news/north-
    east-news/killer-nurse-who-poisoned-patients-
    15636763
66. http://news.bbc.co.uk/2/hi/uk_news/england/
    west_yorkshire/8424131.stm
67. https://www.bbc.com/news/uk-scotland-
    43216615
68. https://www.mylondon.news/news/north-
    london-news/neighbours-notorious-camden-
    ripper-reveal-20736340
69. https://www.telegraph.co.uk/news/1418048/
    Third-bin-bag-murder-victim-named.html
70. https://web.archive.org/web/
    20160508182219/http://news.sky.com/story/
    151680/hardy-charged-with-bin-bag-murders
71. https://web.archive.org/web/
    20140403090108/http://www.crimelibrary.
    com/serial_killers/predators/anthony_hardy/
    2.html
72. https://web.archive.org/web/
    20100628185659/http://www.telegraph.co.uk/
    finance/financetopics/g20-summit/5749486/
    Officer-under-investigation-over-Ian-
    Tomlinsons-death-should-not-have-been-
    working-for-Met.html
73. https://www.mylondon.news/news/west-
    london-news/gruesome-unsolved-murder-
    hounslows-zoe-17601983
74. https://www.chroniclelive.co.uk/news/north-
    east-news/serial-killer-anthony-hardy-dies-
    25305485

75. https://web.archive.org/web/
20121009124159/http://news.sky.com/story/
779866/camden-ripper-will-never-be-let-out

76. https://www.nowtv.com/gb/watch/home/
asset/britains-most-evil-killers/
iYEQYZaTURDhwmVTrCnqGG/seasons/6/
episodes/9/A5EK3PiSkPqtP5YHLK6xN

77. https://www.thetimes.co.uk/

78. https://www.theguardian.com/uk/2006/dec/
20/suffolkmurders.estheraddley

79. https://www.theguardian.com/uk/2008/feb/
21/suffolkmurders.ukcrime1

80. https://www.bbc.co.uk/news/uk-england-
norfolk-41989345

81. https://www.theguardian.com/uk/2008/feb/
22/suffolkmurders.law

82. https://www.dailymotion.com/video/x6ndepx

83. https://www.theguardian.com/uk-news/2021/
sep/24/police-to-re-examine-unsolved-uk-case-
after-21-years-vicky-glass

84. https://www.birminghammail.co.uk/news/
midlands-news/suffolk-strangler-steve-wright-
arrested-21183344

85. http://news.bbc.co.uk/2/hi/uk_news/england/
london/7401250.stm

86. https://www.theguardian.com/uk/2010/may/
27/bradford-murders-timeline

87. https://www.standard.co.uk/news/uk/trial-
date-set-for-bradford-accused-6477642.html

88. https://www.mirror.co.uk/news/uk-news/
crossbow-cannibal-stephen-griffiths-gives-
118864

89. https://www.mirror.co.uk/news/uk-news/
crossbow-cannibal-stephen-griffiths-slashes-
165275

90. https://www.bbc.co.uk/news/10254456
91. https://www.theguardian.com/uk/2010/jun/01/bradford-murders-stephen-griffiths
92. https://www.telegraph.co.uk/news/uknews/crime/8228257/Crossbow-Cannibal-was-a-known-serial-killer-in-the-making.html
93. https://www.telegraph.co.uk/news/uknews/crime/10458065/Female-serial-killer-admits-murdering-three-men-before-dumping-their-bodies-in-ditches.html
94. https://www.theguardian.com/uk-news/2013/nov/18/woman-admits-murdering-men-stabbed-ditches
95. https://www.bbc.com/news/uk-england-cambridgeshire-25825565
96. https://www.theguardian.com/uk-news/2016/mar/18/joanna-dennehy-probation-service-supervision-murders
97. https://www.bbc.com/news/uk-england-cambridgeshire-26192778
98. https://www.theguardian.com/uk-news/2014/feb/28/joanna-dennehy-serial-killer-first-woman-die-in-jail
99. https://www.thetimes.co.uk/article/who-is-lucy-letby-nurse-killed-family-babies-background-family-friends-education-s7njrswmc
100. https://www.bbc.co.uk/programmes/m001q7dl
101. https://www.thetimes.co.uk/article/lucy-letby-files-nurse-hospital-evidence-rkxchgqh9
102. https://news.sky.com/story/lucy-letby-trial-rigid-wire-or-tube-could-have-caused-babys-extraordinary-bleeding-court-told-12750428
103. https://www.telegraph.co.uk/news/2023/08/18/lucy-letby-ian-brady-uk-worst-serial-child-killers/

104. https://www.cps.gov.uk/mersey-cheshire/news/
     lucy-letby-found-guilty-baby-murders
105. https://spot-media.net/2023/04/18/lucy-letby-
     trial-nurses-notes-read-i-killed-them/
106. https://cradleview.net/parallels-of-evil-lucy-
     letby-beverly-allitt-and-the-alarming-potential-
     for-more/
107. https://indiasmagazine.com/lucy-letby-
     biography/
108. https://daybreak.ng/nurse-found-guilty-of-
     murdering-seven-babies-in-her-care/

About the Author

Alan R Warren is a Bestselling Author, Producer, and host of the popular NBC Radioshow *House of Mystery* and *Inside Writing*, both heard on the 106.5 F.M. Los Angeles/102.3 F.M. Riverside/ 1050 A.M. Palm Springs/ 540 A.M. KYAH Salt Lake City/  1150 A.M. KKNW Seattle/Tacoma and Phoenix.

His bestselling true crime books in Canada include *Beyond Suspicion: The True Story of Colonel Russell Williams*, which will be featured on CNN's *Lies, Crimes, & Videos* (Season 4), and *Murder Times Six: The True Story of the Wells Gray Park Murders*. In America, his bestsellers include *The Killing Game: Serial Killer Rodney Alcala*, which was featured on several television shows such as *Very Scary People with Donny Walberg*, Oxygen's *Mark of a Killer*, Reelz' *Killer Trophies*, and soon to be included in a four-part Sundance Channel documentary called *Death's Date*. His bestseller, *Doomsday Cults: The Devil's Hostages*, was featured on Vice's *Dark Side of the '90s*.

His latest series, *Killer Queens*, is a six-part book series covering murders that affect the Gay Community. So far, it includes Book 1 - Leopold & Loeb, Book 2 - Butcher of Hanover: Fritz Haarmann, Book 3 - Grindr Serial Killer: Stephen Port, and Book 4 - Bruce McArthur: Toronto Gay Killer.

Also By Alan R. Warren

Murderous Minds – France

The *International Serial Killers Encyclopedia* series sheds light on the murderous minds of many killers, including their motivations, methods, and madness, through detailed research and explicit retelling of events. Some are notorious names that echo through history books, while others are lesser-known killers whose stories are no less harrowing. Each volume reveals a new layer of darkness.

Monstrous Minds France, Volume 3, takes you deep into the twisted psyches of France's most notorious serial killers. From the grisly scenes of their crimes to the psychological profiles that unravel their motives, this book offers a chilling exploration of evil incarnate. Each chapter unveils a new horror story, detailing the lives, deeds, and capture of these monstrous individuals who left a trail of fear across the French landscape.

Through meticulous research and compelling

narratives, Monstrous Minds France sheds light on the darkness within, leaving readers haunted by the complex web of human depravity and the enduring quest for justice.

Murderous Minds – Soviet Union

The *International Serial Killers Encyclopedia* series sheds light on the murderous minds of many killers, including their motivations, methods, and madness, through detailed research and explicit retelling of events. Some are notorious names that echo through history books, while others are lesser-known killers whose stories are no less harrowing. Each volume reveals a new layer of darkness.

Volume 2 of the series focuses on the most notorious serial killers from the Soviet Union Era of history. In the shadows of the Iron Curtain, amidst the turmoil of revolution and the rigid structures of the Soviet regime, a different kind of darkness lurked. Behind closed doors and beneath the watchful eyes of the state, a breed of killers emerged, their crimes shrouded in secrecy and fear from the haunting corridors of Moscow to the desolate landscapes of Siberia.

From Andrei Chikatilo, a.k.a. the "Butcher of Rostov," whose insatiable hunger for violence claimed the lives of dozens, leaving a trail of mutilation and terror in his wake, to Vasili Komaroff, a.k.a. the "Wolf of Moscow," who killed so many men, he couldn't even remember his kill count. Each chapter reveals the brutal tales of individuals consumed by their darkest desires and a compelling blend of true crime and psychological intrigue.

Murderous Minds Soviet Union delves deeper, revealing the many enigmatic figures who haunted a nation's collective consciousness. Each chapter unveils a new layer of horror and intrigue where the echoes of the past continue to reverberate to this day.

Murderous Minds – Germany

The *International Serial Killers Encyclopedia* series sheds light on the murderous minds of many killers, including their motivations, methods, and madness, through detailed research and explicit retelling of events. Some are notorious names that echo through history books, while others are lesser-known killers whose stories are no less harrowing. Each volume reveals a new layer of darkness.

Volume 1 of the series focuses on the most notorious serial killers from Germany. It contains many cases where the twisted minds and deeds of those who stalked the streets of Germany left a trail of fear and destruction in their wake.

From the infamous Fritz Haarmann, a.k.a. the "Butcher of Hanover," who preyed upon young boys with chilling brutality, to Peter Kürten, a.k.a. the "Vampire of Dusseldorf," whose thirst for blood knew no bounds. Each chapter reveals the brutal tales of individuals consumed by their darkest desires and a compelling blend of true crime and psychological intrigue.

Murderous Minds Germany offers a chilling glimpse into the darkest recesses of the human psyche, reminding us that evil can lurk just beneath the surface, even in the most civilized society.

MURDER TIMES SIX: The True Story of The Wells Park Murders

"The author even had me (who conducted the interview) on the edge of my seat as I was turning the pages as "the Detective" was trying to unearth the unspeakable truth."

Sgt. Mike Eastham R.C.M.P.

It was a crime unlike anything seen in British Columbia. The horror of the "Wells Gray Murders" almost forty years ago transcends decades.

On August 2, 1982, three generations of a family set out on a camping trip – Bob and Jackie Johnson, their two daughters, Janet, 13 and Karen, 11, and Jackie's parents, George and Edith Bentley. A month later, the Johnson family car was found off a mountainside logging road near Wells Gray Park completely burned out. In the back seat were the incinerated remains of four adults, and in the trunk were the two girls.

But this was not just your average mass murder. It was much worse. Over time, some brutal details were revealed; however, most are still only known to the murderer, David Ennis (formerly Shearing). His crimes had far-reaching impacts on the family, community, and country. It still does today. Every time Shearing attempts freedom from the parole board, the grief is triggered as everyone is forced to relive the horrors once again.

Murder Times Six shines a spotlight on the crime that captured the attention of a nation, recounts the narrative of a complex police investigation, and discusses whether a convicted mass murderer should ever be allowed to leave the confines of an institution. Most importantly, it tells the story of one family forever changed.

Beyond Suspicion: Russell Williams – A Canadian Serial Killer

Young girl's panties started to go missing; sexual assaults began to occur, and then female bodies were found! Soon this quiet town of Tweed, Ontario, was in a panic. What is even more shocking was when an upstanding resident stood accused of the assaults. This was not just any man, but a pillar of the community; a decorated military pilot who had flown Canadian Forces VIP aircraft for dignitaries such as the Queen of England, Prince Philip, the Governor-General and Prime Minister of Canada.

This is the story of serial killer Russell Williams, the elite pilot of Canada's Air Force One, and the innocent victims he murdered. Unlike other serial killers, Williams seemed very unaffected about his crimes and leading two different lives.

Alan R. Warren describes the secret life including the abductions, rape, and murders that were unleashed on an unsuspecting community. Included are letters written to the victims by Williams and descriptions of the assaults and rapes as seen on videos and photos taken by Williams during the attacks.

This updated version also contains the full brilliant police interrogation of Williams and his confession. Also, the twisted way the Williams planned to pin his crimes on his unsuspecting neighbor.

Doomsday Cults: The Devil's Hostages

Jim Jones convinced his 1000 followers they would all have to commit suicide since he was going to die. Shoko Asahara convinced his followers to release a weapon of mass destruction, the deadly sarin gas, on a Tokyo

subway. The Order of the Solar Temple lured the rich and famous, including Princess Grace of Monaco, and convinced them to die a fiery death now on Earth to be reborn on a better planet called Sirius. Charles Manson convinced his followers to kill, in an attempt to incite an apocalyptic race war.

These are a few of the doomsday cults examined in this book by bestselling author Alan R. Warren. Its focus is on cults whose destructive behavior was due in large part to their apocalyptic beliefs or doomsday movements. It includes details surrounding the massacres and a look into how their members became so brainwashed they committed unimaginable crimes at the command of their leader.

Usually, when we hear about these cults and their massacres, we ask ourselves how it possibly happened. We could also ask ourselves, what then is the difference between a cult and a religion? We once had a small group of people who unquestionably followed a person who believed he was the son of God. Two thousand years later, that following is one of the most recognized religions in the world. This book in no way criticizes believing in God. Rather, it examines how a social movement grows into a full religion and when it does not. And what makes the conventional faiths such as Christianity, Judaism, Islam, and Hinduism stand above groups such as the Branch Davidians or Children of God.

In Chains: The Dangerous World of Human Trafficking

Human trafficking is the trade of people for forced labor or sex. It also includes the illegal extraction of human organs and tissues. And it is an extremely ruthless and dangerous industry plaguing our world today.

Most believe human trafficking occurs in countries with no human rights legislation. This is a myth. All types of human trafficking are alive and well in most of the developed countries of the world, like the United States, Canada, and the UK. It is estimated that $150 billion a year is generated in the forced labor industry alone. It is also believed that 21 million people are trapped in modern-day slavery – exploited for sex, labor, or organs.

Most also believe since they live in a free country, there

is built-in protection against such illegal practices. But for many, this is not the case. Traffickers tend to focus on the most vulnerable in our society, but trafficking can happen to anyone. You will see how easy it can happen in the stories included in "In Chains."

BUTCHER OF HANOVER: Fritz Haarmann (Killer Queens 2)

Killer Queens is a new series of historical fiction books based on true stories. Sources, such as police reports and newspaper articles, are examined to gather as many facts as possible surrounding each case. As with any work of fiction, some creative additions are made when telling these stories, usually within the conversations between the personalities involved. The various sources are the basis of these conversations and hopefully, make them come alive for the readers to help understand what was meant by those words.

Book 2 of the series focuses on the serial killer of at least twenty-seven young men and boys in Germany in the post-World War I era. At the center of this murder case were Fritz Haarmann and Hans Grans, who were lovers while committing these murders. It wasn't until the skulls and bones started washing ashore from the Leine River in Hanover that Germany realized they had a cold-blooded serial killer in their country.

Unlike Leopold and Loeb murder case covered in Book 1, where the dominance shifted from one to the other, Fritz Haarmann was the dominant partner in this case. He carried out each of the murders and dismemberment of the bodies himself, even though he claimed that Grans chose who was to be murdered in court.

As you read the exploration of the case in this book, ask yourself, did Haarmann murder each victim to keep his lover Hans Grans to stay with him? Did Grans decide who it was that was to be murdered? The evidence on this case will keep you on the edge of your seat, trying to determine who was really behind these gruesome murders.

www.ingramcontent.com/pod-product-compliance
Lightning Source LLC
Chambersburg PA
CBHW070915120626
46546CB00001B/269